# HUDDERSFIELD NARROW CANAL
## A Towpath Guide

# NOTES

# HUDDERSFIELD NARROW CANAL
## A Towpath Guide

A guide to walking the Huddersfield Narrow Canal
including part of the Ashton Canal

Dr Bob Gough

## Huddersfield Canal Society

Published by:

Huddersfield Canal Society
Transhipment Warehouse
Wool Road
Dobcross
Oldham
OL3 5QR

© Huddersfield Canal Society 2008
Reprinted with amendments 2009

ISBN 978-0-9514270-1-9

*Printed by:*
Kelvin Print Group, Rexcine Way,
Hyde, Cheshire, SK14 4GX

# CONTENTS

Acknowledgements ................................... 8
Foreword ................................................ 9
Introduction ........................................... 10
Huddersfield Narrow Canal ................... 12
Maps & Views
    Portland Basin, Ashton-u-Lyne ............ 14
    Lock 1W, Whitelands Road ................ 16
    Whitelands Industrial Estate................. 18
    Tame Aqueduct & Staley Wharf .......... 20
    Stalybridge Town Centre ..................... 22
    North End Road .................................. 24
    Grove Road, Millbrook ....................... 26
    Heyrod ............................................... 28
    Scout Tunnel ...................................... 30
    Mossley Bottoms ............................... 32
    Woodend, Mossley ............................ 34
    Roaches, Mossley .............................. 36
    Manns Wharf Bridge ......................... 38
    Shaw Hall Bank, Greenfield ................ 40
    Frenches, Uppermill ........................... 42
    Uppermill High Street ......................... 44
    Wool Road, Dobcross ......................... 46

Diggle Flight ......................................... 48
Diggle Portal ......................................... 50
Standedge Moor, Diggle ...................... 52
Standedge Moor, Marsden ................. 54
Tunnel End, Marsden .......................... 56
Marsden Town Centre ......................... 58
Sparth Reservoir .................................. 60
Lingards Wood ..................................... 62
West Slaithwaite .................................. 64
Slaithwaite Town Centre ..................... 66
Platt Lane, Slaithwaite ......................... 68
Linthwaite ............................................ 70
Lowestwood ......................................... 72
Golcar Aqueduct .................................. 74
Milnsbridge ......................................... 76
West Paddock ....................................... 78
Longroyd Bridge .................................. 80
Manchester Road ................................. 82
Lock 1E, Huddersfield University ......... 84
Huddersfield Canal Society ..................... 86
Further Information ............................... 87
Distance Tables ...................................... 88

**Disclaimer:**

*Every effort has been made to check the accuracy of the information in this Guide.*
*However, the Huddersfield Canal Society cannot be held liable for any losses arising from*
*errors, omissions or otherwise, in using this Guide to explore the Canal and its surroundings.*
*It should not be assumed the paths depicted on the maps are public rights of way.*

## ACKNOWLEDGEMENTS

It has been a fascinating venture producing this new Towpath Guide as part of my work as Administrator at the Huddersfield Canal Society.

I am indebted to the Chairman, Neville Kenyon, and the Council of Management for supporting the project.

There have been many discussions with family, friends and members of the Canal Society whose help and encouragement is gratefully acknowledged.

Each time I visit the Canal, it seems there are always new things to see; whether through the changing seasons, new canal-side developments or simply looking more closely.

I hope this Guide will inspire you to get out on the Canal and see for yourself!

Bob Gough

February 2008

8

# FOREWORD

The so-called 'Canalmania' at the turn of the 18th century created an extensive network of over 3,600 miles of inland navigations. However, the railways and then motor transport led to their gradual decline and abandonment. Canals became unusable, unpleasant and more often than not, a local dumping ground.

Fortunately, a small group of enthusiasts in the 1940s campaigned to arrest the neglect of the remaining network. Their progress was slow at first, but in recent years, with substantial investment, canals have undergone a remarkable renaissance. No longer unsafe and unattractive, they are now a valuable local and national recreational resource, free for all to explore and enjoy.

The Huddersfield Narrow exemplifies this transformation. With a wealth of natural beauty and architectural heritage, not to mention colourful narrowboats navigating the waterway, there can be no better way of enjoying the Narrow on foot and this Guide is the perfect companion.

Robin Evans
*British Waterways*
*Chief Executive*

# INTRODUCTION

The Huddersfield Canal Society first published a Towpath Guide in 1981. It was chiefly text-based, accompanied by sketch maps, and included articles on canal history, plant and animal life, engineering and a good pub guide! The narrative described a walk from Cooper Bridge on the Huddersfield Broad, along the Huddersfield Narrow and part of the Ashton Canal as far as Dukinfield Junction at Portland Basin near where it meets the Upper Peak Forest Canal.

This East - West approach has an unfortunate consequence for the accompanying maps which can appear inverted, cartographically, with North pointing downwards, and furthermore, the text is difficult to follow should you be walking in the opposite (West to East) direction. Nonetheless, it provides a fascinating insight into the Huddersfield Canals at a time when Society volunteers were starting their restoration work at Dungebooth Lock (22W) in Uppermill.

Since the Huddersfield Narrow re-opened to full navigation in May 2001, there has been a need for a new Guide. From the outset, it was decided to take an illustrative approach, dispensing with a formal narrative, thereby making a Guide which, it is hoped, will be easy to use when walking in either a westerly or easterly direction. Portland Basin (Ashton-under-Lyne) in the West and Aspley Basin (Huddersfield), in the East, have been taken as limits for the Guide.

Each map covers about 0.8km (0.5mi) of canal (except Standedge Moor which is covered in two 3.2km (2.0mi) sections) and the accompanying photos show the sequence of towpath views when walking easterly toward Huddersfield and westerly toward Ashton. The camera symbols ( A ) indicate the locations from which the views were taken. Unless denoted by the symbol (⊘), any road or track crossing the canal will allow you to get on or off the towpath ( ---- ).

The depiction of trees/scrub (  ) and buildings (   ) is not intended to be definitive, but gives an impression of the local scenery you will experience. The wider scene is also indicated ( ). The walking surface and amount of puddles are shown in broad categories and represent the *range* of conditions in each section; the 'overgrown' condition ( ) includes a worn out, as well as an un-surfaced, towpath. The featured items of interest may either be seen along that particular section of canal ( ) or apply generally (no symbol); photographs from the Canal Society's archive are shown by the symbol ( ).

Crossing Standedge Moor is not to be taken lightly. The weather on the Moor is notoriously changeable; paths can be boggy when wet and areas may have no signal for mobile phone networks. A detailed guide and Moor-centred Ordnance Survey® map are available from the Marsden Information Point, Peel Street, Marsden (01484 845595).

As two alternative routes across Standedge Moor are shown, the views have been reduced to two sets of three photographs in either direction, giving a flavour of the scenery you will encounter. If you do not wish to walk across the Moor, there are buses available (Traveline 0871 200 2323 *www.traveline.org.uk*). The more adventurous may like to join the convoy of boats when they are towed through Standedge Tunnel. Foot passengers may purchase a 'Hiker's Ticket'; contact British Waterways (01977 554351) for more details.

Always take care when walking by the Huddersfield Narrow, or any canal; especially near Locks. Walking in company is not only safer, but more enjoyable through a shared experience.

*Note: The indication of facilities such as pubs, cafés, restaurants, etc. on the maps does not imply any endorsement by the Huddersfield Canal Society.*

# HUDDERSFIELD NARROW CANAL

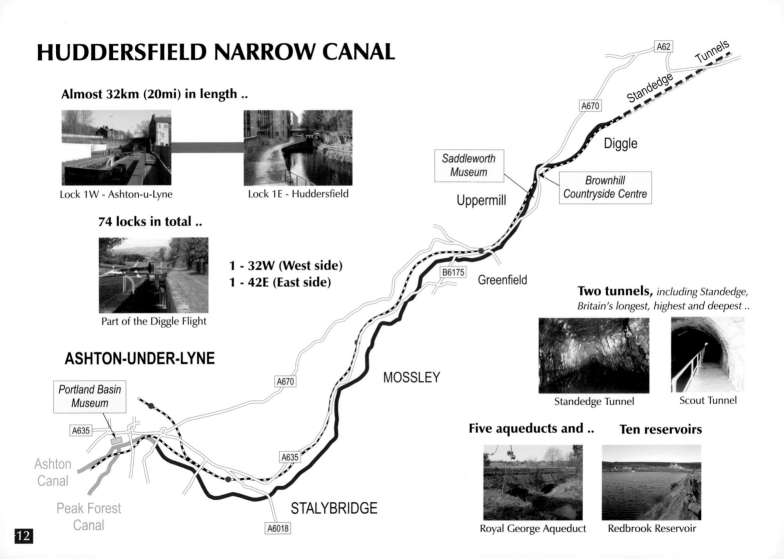

**Almost 32km (20mi) in length ..**

Lock 1W - Ashton-u-Lyne

Lock 1E - Huddersfield

**74 locks in total ..**

1 - 32W (West side)
1 - 42E (East side)

Part of the Diggle Flight

**ASHTON-UNDER-LYNE**

Portland Basin Museum

A635

Ashton Canal

Peak Forest Canal

A670

A635

MOSSLEY

STALYBRIDGE

A6018

Saddleworth Museum

Uppermill

Greenfield

B6175

Brownhill Countryside Centre

Diggle

Standedge Tunnels

A62

A670

**Two tunnels,** including Standedge, Britain's longest, highest and deepest ..

Standedge Tunnel

Scout Tunnel

**Five aqueducts and ..**

Royal George Aqueduct

**Ten reservoirs**

Redbrook Reservoir

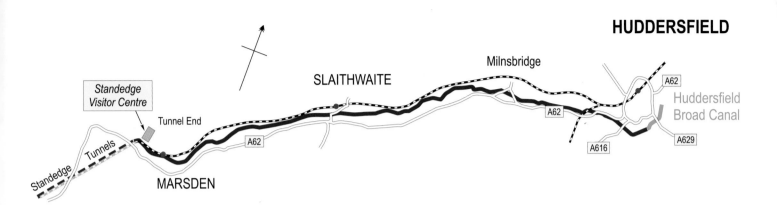

**HUDDERSFIELD**

Milnsbridge

SLAITHWAITE

*Standedge
Visitor Centre*

Tunnel End

Huddersfield
Broad Canal

A62

A62

A616

A629

Standedge Tunnels

MARSDEN

Km

Mi

| | 0 | 1 | 2 | 3 |
| 0 | 1 | 2 |

## Notable Dates

**4 Apr 1794**

Act of Parliament passed to authorise construction of the Huddersfield Narrow Canal

**4 Apr 1811**

Completion of Standedge Tunnel and official opening of the Narrow Canal

**21 Dec 1944**

Canal abandoned by the London Midland & Scottish Railways (Canals) Act

**19 Apr 1974**

Huddersfield Canal Society formed to campaign for the restoration of the Canal

**26 Mar 1986**

£1.2m grant paid to the Society from the abolition of Greater Manchester Council

**29 Jul 1988**

British Waterways (No 2) Act passed allowing boats to navigate the Canal again

**13 Dec 1996**

Major grant from Millennium Commission; matching funds from English Partnerships

**1 May 2001**

Huddersfield Narrow Canal again open to complete through navigation

**3 Sep 2001**

Huddersfield Narrow Canal officially re-opened by HRH Prince Charles

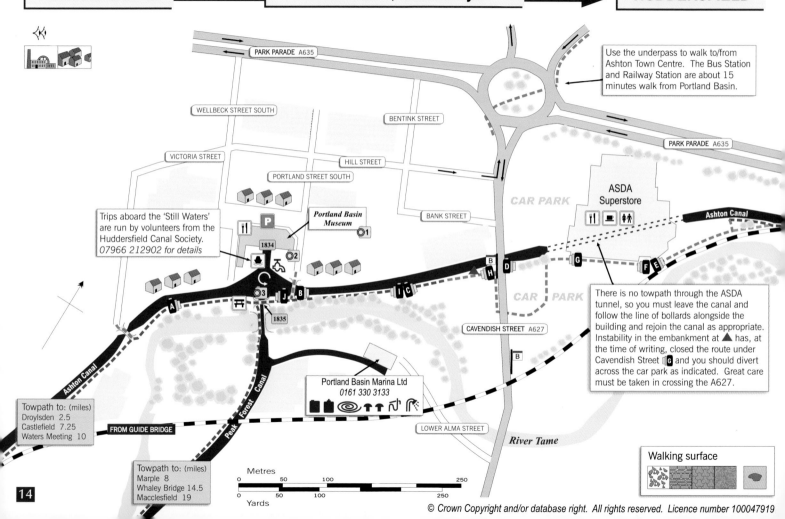

PARK PARADE A635

WELLBECK STREET SOUTH

BENTINK STREET

VICTORIA STREET

HILL STREET

PORTLAND STREET SOUTH

BANK STREET

PARK PARADE A635

Use the underpass to walk to/from Ashton Town Centre. The Bus Station and Railway Station are about 15 minutes walk from Portland Basin.

ASDA Superstore

CAR PARK

Ashton Canal

*Portland Basin Museum* 1

Trips aboard the 'Still Waters' are run by volunteers from the Huddersfield Canal Society. *07966 212902 for details*

1834

2

B H D

G

F E

3 J B

C

CAR PARK

There is no towpath through the ASDA tunnel, so you must leave the canal and follow the line of bollards alongside the building and rejoin the canal as appropriate. Instability in the embankment at ▲ has, at the time of writing, closed the route under Cavendish Street G and you should divert across the car park as indicated. Great care must be taken in crossing the A627.

A

1835

CAVENDISH STREET A627

B

Ashton Canal

Portland Basin Marina Ltd
0161 330 3133

Peak Forest Canal

FROM GUIDE BRIDGE

LOWER ALMA STREET

*River Tame*

Towpath to: (miles)
Droylsden 2.5
Castlefield 7.25
Waters Meeting 10

Towpath to: (miles)
Marple 8
Whaley Bridge 14.5
Macclesfield 19

Metres
0   50   100   250

Yards
0   50   100   250

Walking surface

14

### Portland Basin Museum  `1834` `○1`

Step back in time and experience the lifestyle, industries, crafts and trades of previous generations of Tamesiders.

0161 343 2878
Free Admission

### The Waterwheel  `○2`

The old warehouse at Portland Basin (burned down in 1972 and rebuilt as Portland Basin Museum) had water-powered hoists which were driven by this 'undershot' waterwheel; water ran from the canal, under the wheel and discharged into the river Tame.

### Stone arch footbridge  `1835` `○3`

Spanning part of the Ashton canal, this elegant, stone-built footbridge became notorious for many attempted suicides during the Cotton Famine of the 1860's and hence the canal basin in the foreground gained the nickname 'The Weaver's Rest'.

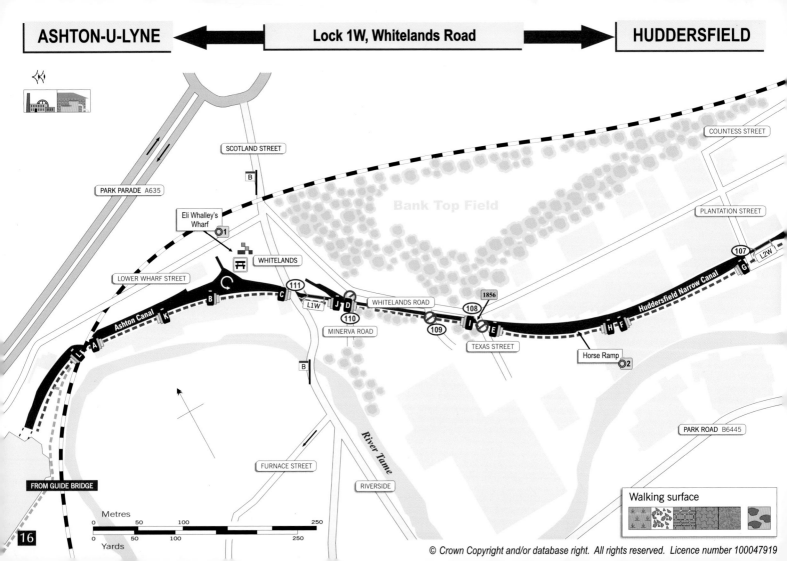

SCOTLAND STREET

PARK PARADE A635

COUNTESS STREET

PLANTATION STREET

Eli Whalley's Wharf ⊙1

Bank Top Field

WHITELANDS

LOWER WHARF STREET

107 L2W

G

111

Huddersfield Narrow Canal

L1W

J D

WHITELANDS ROAD

1856

108

B

Ashton Canal

K

110

MINERVA ROAD

109

I E

H F

TEXAS STREET

L A

Horse Ramp ⊙2

B

PARK ROAD B6445

FURNACE STREET

River Tame

FROM GUIDE BRIDGE

RIVERSIDE

Metres
0    50    100         250

Yards
0    50    100    250

**16**

**Walking surface**

### Eli Whalley's or Donkey Stone Wharf ①

Former site of the last manufacturer of 'Donkey stones' - Gilbert Garside & Son. These hard 'stones' were made in brown, cream and white varieties and used by proud housewives to treat their front steps, cills and flag pavements.

### Horse Ramp ②

Despite the sure-footedness of boat horses, there were occasions when some would fall into the canal, especially when un-nerved by steam trains passing along the nearby line. This submerged ramp was built to help horses safely out of the canal.

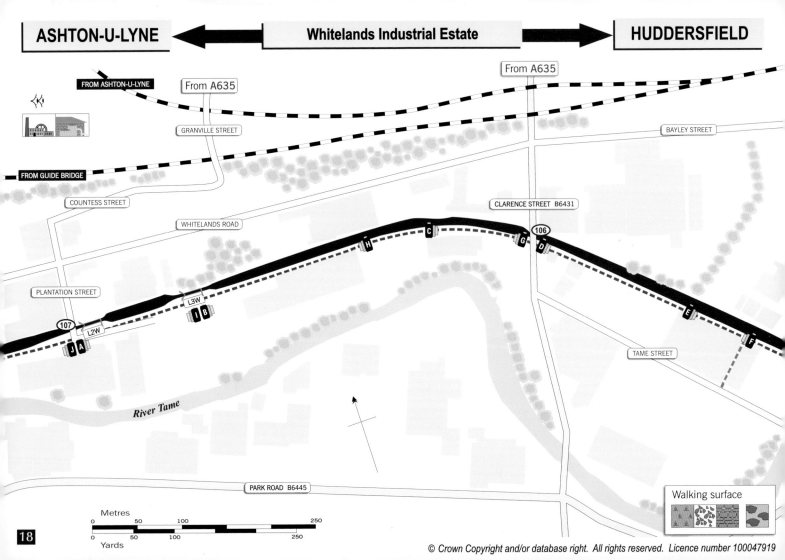

ASHTON-U-LYNE ← Whitelands Industrial Estate → HUDDERSFIELD

From A635

FROM ASHTON-U-LYNE

From A635

GRANVILLE STREET

BAYLEY STREET

FROM GUIDE BRIDGE

COUNTESS STREET

CLARENCE STREET B6431

WHITELANDS ROAD

H

C

106

G
D

PLANTATION STREET

L3W

107

I   B

E

L2W

J   A

F

TAME STREET

River Tame

PARK ROAD B6445

Walking surface

Metres
0    50    100    250

18

Yards
0    50    100    250

© Crown Copyright and/or database right. All rights reserved. Licence number 100047919

### Winching Roller

The maintenance and repair of the canal depended on being able to drain sections and this dumbell-shaped winch was used to lift a plug in the canal bed. The plug is usually situated above a stream or culvert to carry the water away safely. You will pass many such winches walking the towpath.

### Stop Plank Grooves

These pairs of grooves cut into the washwall masonry are used to locate a number of timber 'stop planks' which, when slotted in one above another, form a temporary dam. Another set of planks nearby would allow the enclosed section to be drained whilst maintaining the water level beyond for navigation.

### Strengthening Masonry

Courses of masonry capping bridges and aqueducts were often strengthened by joining the blocks with large iron 'staples'. The ironwork was secured in place by cutting oversize holes in the stones, part-filling the cavities with molten lead and quickly hammering the 'staple' home.

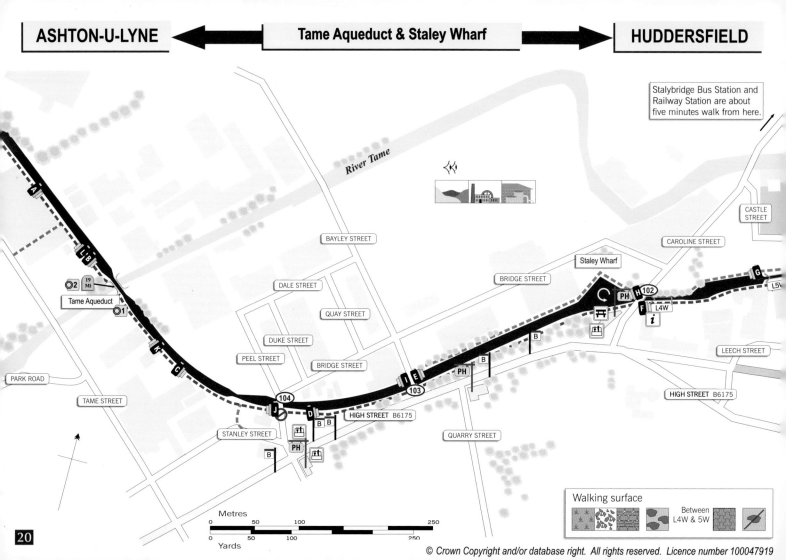

ASHTON-U-LYNE ← Tame Aqueduct & Staley Wharf → HUDDERSFIELD

Stalybridge Bus Station and Railway Station are about five minutes walk from here.

River Tame

CASTLE STREET

BAYLEY STREET

CAROLINE STREET

Staley Wharf

BRIDGE STREET

DALE STREET

2   19 Mi

Tame Aqueduct   1

QUAY STREET

PH   102

L4W

F

i

DUKE STREET

PEEL STREET

BRIDGE STREET

LEECH STREET

PARK ROAD

TAME STREET

104

HIGH STREET B6175

HIGH STREET B6175

J

STANLEY STREET

B   B

PH

QUARRY STREET

B

PH

Metres
0   50   100   250

Yards
0   50   100   250

20

Walking surface

Between L4W & 5W

© Crown Copyright and/or database right. All rights reserved. Licence number 100047919

### Aqueduct over the River Tame ⦾1

Consisting of a cast iron trough carrying the canal and a separate stone arch for the towpath, it was built in 1801, replacing an original structure destroyed by a flood in August 1799. The towpath arch collapsed and was rebuilt several times. Later strengthening work linked the arch and trough with a strut c1875.

### 19mi Milestone ⦾2

The stone arch wall, doubling in height midway on the aqueduct, contains the 19mi milestone, with a benchmark, and the oval outline of a London & North Western Railway bridge plate (No. 105).

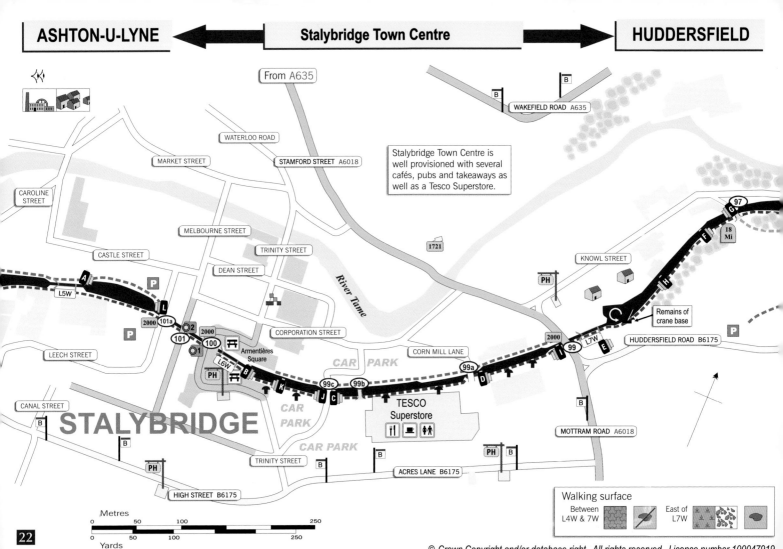

ASHTON-U-LYNE ← | Stalybridge Town Centre | → HUDDERSFIELD

From A635

WATERLOO ROAD

MARKET STREET

STAMFORD STREET A6018

CAROLINE STREET

MELBOURNE STREET

TRINITY STREET

CASTLE STREET

DEAN STREET

Stalybridge Town Centre is well provisioned with several cafés, pubs and takeaways as well as a Tesco Superstore.

WAKEFIELD ROAD A635

B
B

97
G
I8 Mi
F

KNOWL STREET

H

L5W
A
L
101a
2000
2
101
100
2000
L6W
PH
B
K
J
C
99c
99b
99a
D

River Tame

1721

CORPORATION STREET

Armentières Square

CORN MILL LANE

CAR PARK

PH
L7W
E
2000
99
I

Remains of crane base

HUDDERSFIELD ROAD B6175

P

LEECH STREET

CANAL STREET

STALYBRIDGE

CAR PARK

CAR PARK

TESCO Superstore

MOTTRAM ROAD A6018

B

PH
B

TRINITY STREET

B

ACRES LANE B6175

PH
B

HIGH STREET B6175

Walking surface
Between L4W & 7W
East of L7W

Metres
0    50    100              250
0    50    100         250
Yards

22

### Stalybridge Restoration - I

Restoring the canal through Stalybridge town centre was a major engineering project, with three out of the four original locks relocated. A 22 tonne box culvert is being lowered into position as part of the service road for Armentières Square.

### Stalybridge Restoration - II

Though much of the canal through the town had to rebuilt from scratch, parts of the original line had survived the infilling of the 1960s. When excavated, Melbourne Street Bridge was found to be in reasonable condition, though the towpath and washwalls had to be rebuilt.

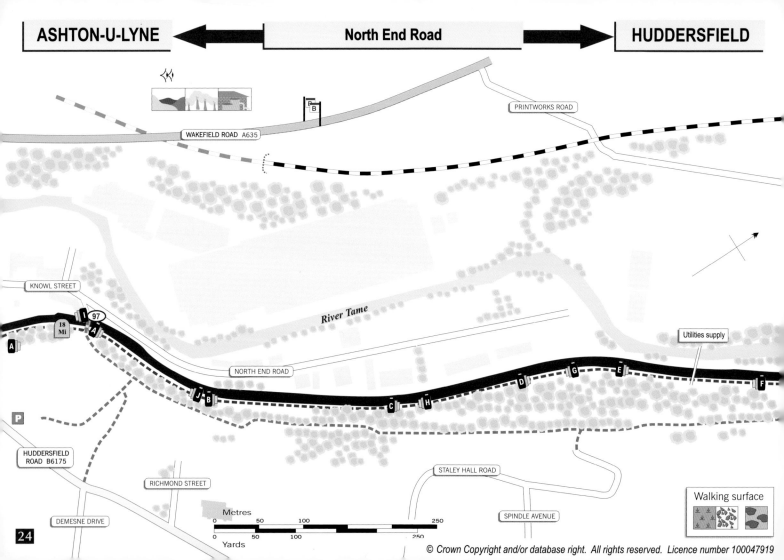

ASHTON-U-LYNE ⟵ North End Road ⟶ HUDDERSFIELD

PRINTWORKS ROAD

WAKEFIELD ROAD A635

River Tame

Utilities supply

KNOWL STREET

97

18 Mi

NORTH END ROAD

P

HUDDERSFIELD ROAD B6175

RICHMOND STREET

STALEY HALL ROAD

Metres
0    50    100    250

Yards
0    50    100    250

DEMESNE DRIVE

SPINDLE AVENUE

Walking surface

24

### Arrowhead

With glossy, arrow-head shaped aerial leaves and spikes of white flowers, Arrowhead *(Sagittaria sagittifolia)* is an easily recognised water plant.
The flowers are described as monoecious, either male or female, though both can appear on the same spike - a female flower is illustrated.

### Flowering Rush

Despite its common name, it is not actually a Rush!  The narrow leaves, often with a twist at their end, look a little rush-like, but the clusters of pink, bitter almond scented, flowers are very distinctive.  The flowers are arranged in so-called umbels, reflected in the plant's Latin name, *Butomus umbellatus.*

### Branched Bur-reed

A robust reed, the Branched Burr-reed *(Sparganium erectum)* has bright green leaves with a distinct ridge or keel along their length.  The flowers are monoecious; the male and female clearly seen on the flowering spike.  The smaller, fluffy male flowers are above the larger, spiky females which ripen to produce hooked seeds.

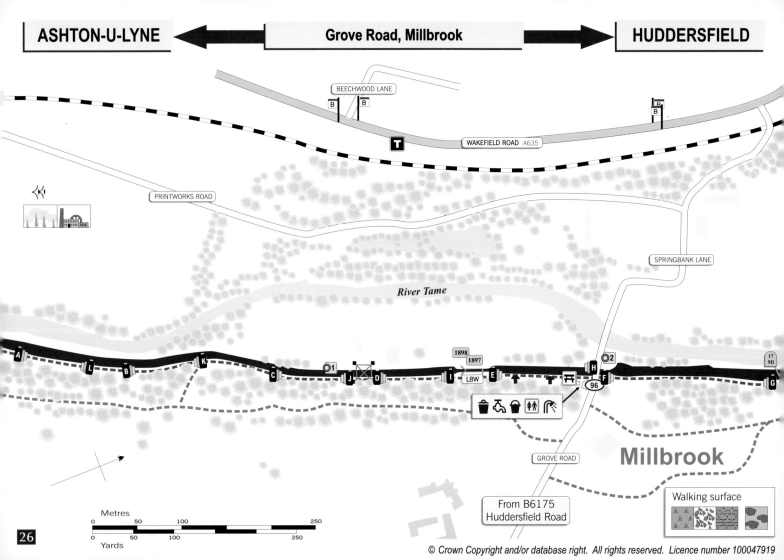

ASHTON-U-LYNE ← Grove Road, Millbrook → HUDDERSFIELD

BEECHWOOD LANE

WAKEFIELD ROAD A635

PRINTWORKS ROAD

SPRINGBANK LANE

River Tame

1898
1897

L8W

17 Mi

96

GROVE ROAD

Millbrook

From B6175
Huddersfield Road

Walking surface

Metres
0    50    100                    250

Yards
0    50    100                    250

26

### Colonising Pond Weed   ⊙1

The rather sterile sheet piled section of canal, which passes between the legs of an electricity pylon, shows signs of plant life with the vigorous growth of Long-stalked Pondweed *(Potamogeton praelongus).*

### Swing Bridge remains   ⊙2

Grove Road bridge was formerly a swing bridge and the modern bridge provides a good vantage point to see the remains of the original bearing plate on the off-side of the canal.

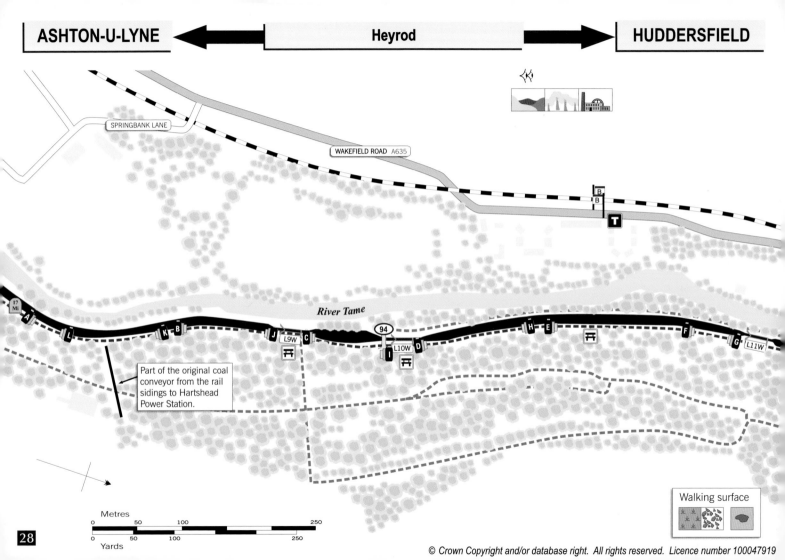

ASHTON-U-LYNE ← Heyrod → HUDDERSFIELD

SPRINGBANK LANE

WAKEFIELD ROAD A635

River Tame

Part of the original coal conveyor from the rail sidings to Hartshead Power Station.

Metres
0   50   100   250

Yards
0   50   100   250

Walking surface

28

### Butterflies - The Comma

In the Summer months, many different types of butterfly may be seen as you walk the towpath, including: Peacock, Red Admiral, Orange Tip, Large White, Small Tortoishell, Speckled Wood and, pictured, the Comma. It gets its name from the white, comma-shaped, mark on the underwing.

### Cinnabar Moth Caterpillars

The yellow, daisy-like, flowered Ragwort is a common plant along the towpath and during the early Summer is often covered with Cinnabar Moth larvae. The plant contains poisons, but the larvae are unaffected and in fact store them for their own defence; their black and orange colours are a warning!

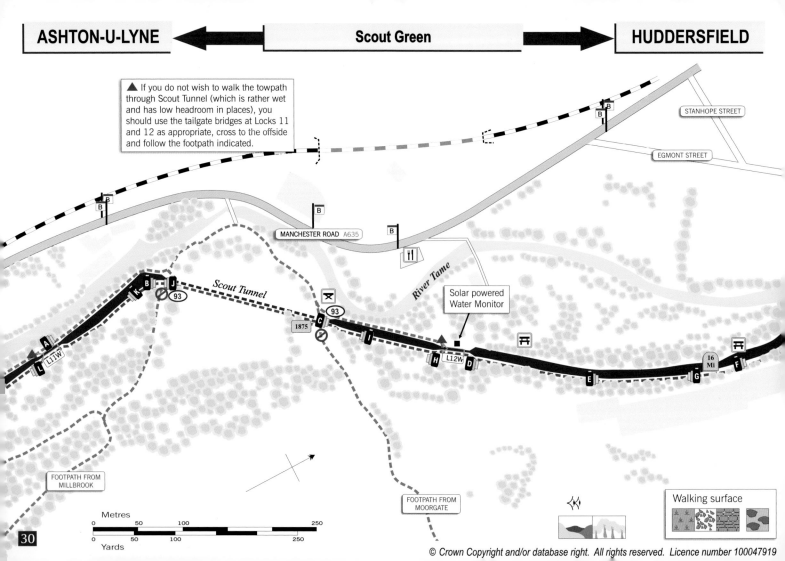

ASHTON-U-LYNE ← Scout Green → HUDDERSFIELD

▲ If you do not wish to walk the towpath through Scout Tunnel (which is rather wet and has low headroom in places), you should use the tailgate bridges at Locks 11 and 12 as appropriate, cross to the offside and follow the footpath indicated.

STANHOPE STREET

EGMONT STREET

B

B

B

MANCHESTER ROAD A635

B

River Tame

Scout Tunnel

K B J
93

1875 C 93

Solar powered
Water Monitor

A

L L11W

H L12W D

I

E G

16
Mi

F

FOOTPATH FROM
MILLBROOK

FOOTPATH FROM
MOORGATE

Metres
0    50    100    250

Yards
0    50    100    250

30

Walking surface

**A**

**B**

**C**

**D**

## Birds - Grey Heron

'Feeding the ducks', and ever-present Canada Geese, is so much a tradition, it is easy to forget the variety of bird life on the canal. Though the dazzling Kingfisher is occasionally seen, more typical are the Grey Heron and Moorhen.

## Moorhen

The Moorhen has a yellow-tipped, red beak and is rather secretive amongst the reeds. The Coot (inset) is more often seen, but its white beak and white 'shield' above the beak easily distinguishes it from the Moorhen.

**F**

**E**

**L**

**K**

**G**

**H**

**I**

**J**

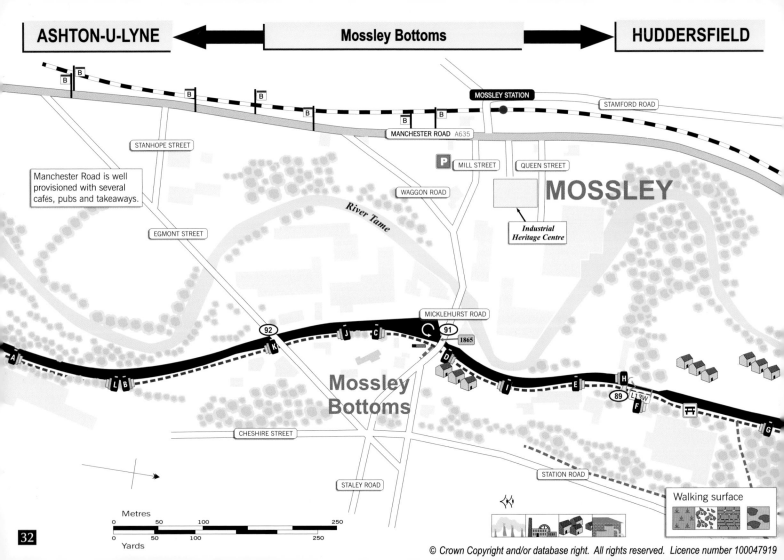

ASHTON-U-LYNE ← **Mossley Bottoms** → HUDDERSFIELD

MOSSLEY STATION

STAMFORD ROAD

MANCHESTER ROAD A635

STANHOPE STREET

**P** MILL STREET QUEEN STREET

Manchester Road is well provisioned with several cafés, pubs and takeaways.

WAGGON ROAD

**MOSSLEY**

*River Tame*

EGMONT STREET

*Industrial Heritage Centre*

MICKLEHURST ROAD

92  J  C  91  1865

K  D

A

L  B  I  E  H

**Mossley Bottoms**  89  L13W  F

CHESHIRE STREET  G

STATION ROAD

STALEY ROAD

**Metres**
0    50    100    250

0    50    100    250
**Yards**

Walking surface

32

© Crown Copyright and/or database right. All rights reserved. Licence number 100047919

### Trees - Goat Willow

Walking the towpath is an ideal way to see many species of Britain's trees, including: Oak, Ash, Beech, Lime, Elm, Poplar, Birch, Hazel, Hawthorn, Maple, Larch etc. but most characteristic of waterside locations are Willow and Alder. The Goat Willow is a delight in Spring as one of the 'pussy willows'.

### Alder

The Alder has blunt, heart-shaped leaves and female catkins ripening to cone-like structures which may persist until the following year (inset). Alder's timber is used to make traditional clogs and its charcoal prized for making the best quality gunpowder!

13W

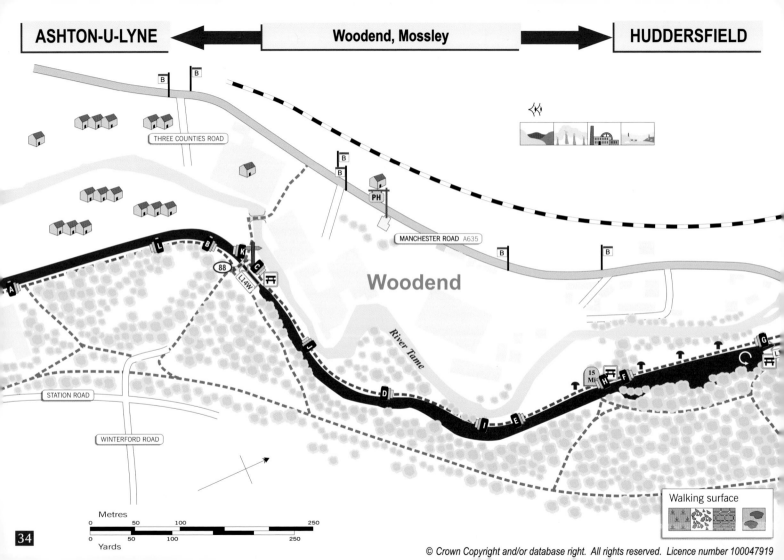

ASHTON-U-LYNE ← Woodend, Mossley → HUDDERSFIELD

THREE COUNTIES ROAD

B
B
PH

MANCHESTER ROAD A635

Woodend

River Tame

88
LLW

STATION ROAD

WINTERFORD ROAD

15 Mi

Metres
0    50    100                                    250
Yards
0    50    100                                    250

34

Walking surface

## Damsels and .....

Canals are an ideal habitat for both damselflies and dragonflies. Their larvae can spend up to three years in the water and are voracious predators. When fully grown, they climb out of the water, pupate and hatch out as winged adults during the summer months. Damselflies and dragonflies are easily

## ..... Dragons

told apart; damselflies usually rest with their wings closed against their bodies, whereas dragonflies rest with their wings outstretched. The intense blue Azure damselfly is most commonly seen, but look out for the Large Red *(pictured)* with its beaded body. The dragonfly shown is a Wide Bodied Chaser.

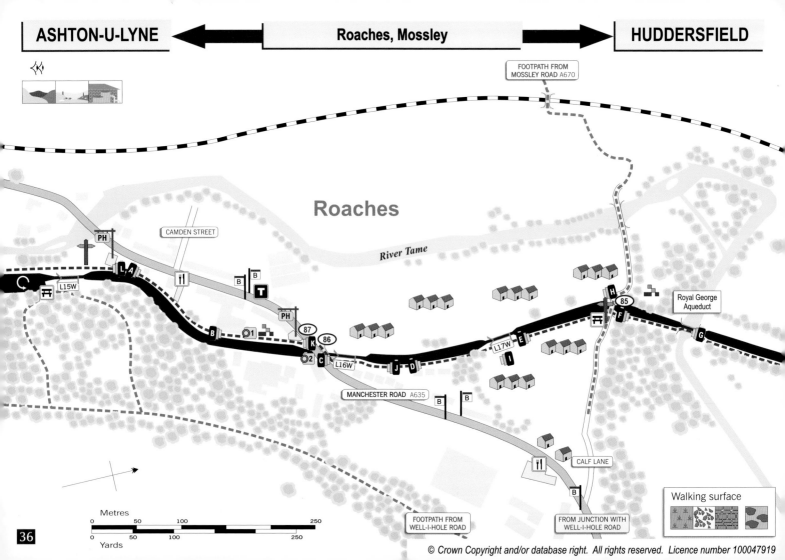

ASHTON-U-LYNE ⬅️ **Roaches, Mossley** ➡️ HUDDERSFIELD

FOOTPATH FROM
MOSSLEY ROAD A670

Roaches

CAMDEN STREET

River Tame

PH

L15W

L A

B

T

PH

87

86

B

K

C

L16W

2

1

J D

L17W E

I

H

85

F

G

Royal George
Aqueduct

MANCHESTER ROAD A635

B

B

CALF LANE

B

FOOTPATH FROM
WELL-I-HOLE ROAD

FROM JUNCTION WITH
WELL-I-HOLE ROAD

Metres
0    50    100                              250

Yards
0    50    100                              250

36

Walking surface

### The Mystery of CBW ◎1

Between Locks 15 & 16W, in the towpath wall, are three blocks of stone each bearing the letters CBW. The C and W are incised, whereas the B, a metal casting, was added later. At least ten examples are known along the canal, so keep your eyes open! Their true meaning is, at present, a mystery.

### Lifting Heavy Stones - I ◎2

The coping stones below Manchester Road bridge show an ingenious method of lifting blocks of masonry. The slot in each stone was used to locate a set of wedges known as a Lewis Pin which, when raised by a shackle, expanded, gripping the stone and allowing it to be lifted and manoeuvred freely.

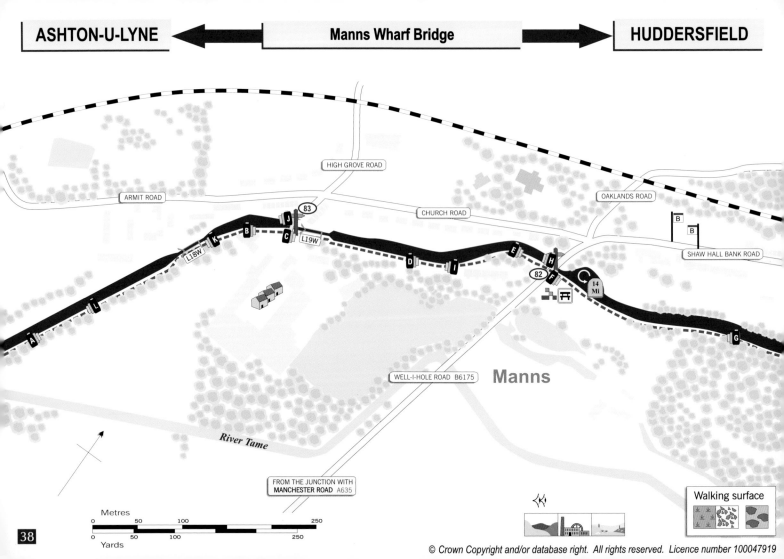

ASHTON-U-LYNE ⟵ Manns Wharf Bridge ⟶ HUDDERSFIELD

HIGH GROVE ROAD

ARMIT ROAD

OAKLANDS ROAD

83

CHURCH ROAD

J

B

K

C

L19W

D

I

E

H

82

F

14 Mi

G

A

L

SHAW HALL BANK ROAD

B

B

L18W

WELL-I-HOLE ROAD B6175

**Manns**

River Tame

FROM THE JUNCTION WITH
**MANCHESTER ROAD** A635

Walking surface

Metres
0   50   100   250

Yards
0   50   100   250

38

### *Alien Invaders - Himalayan Balsam & Japanese Knotweed*

The Himalayan Balsam or 'Policeman's Helmet', named after the shape of its showy flowers, has found the damp canal environs the perfect habitat. Unfortunately, its extensive growth overwhelms our native flora and its persistent, fertile seeds make it difficult to manage.  More pernicious is the Japanese Knotweed which readily forms extensive thickets and its canopy of leaves shades out our native plants early in the Spring. Although its flowers do not produce seed, it can propagate from very small pieces of the plant.  Both the Balsam and Knotweed, being alien introductions, have no natural controls.

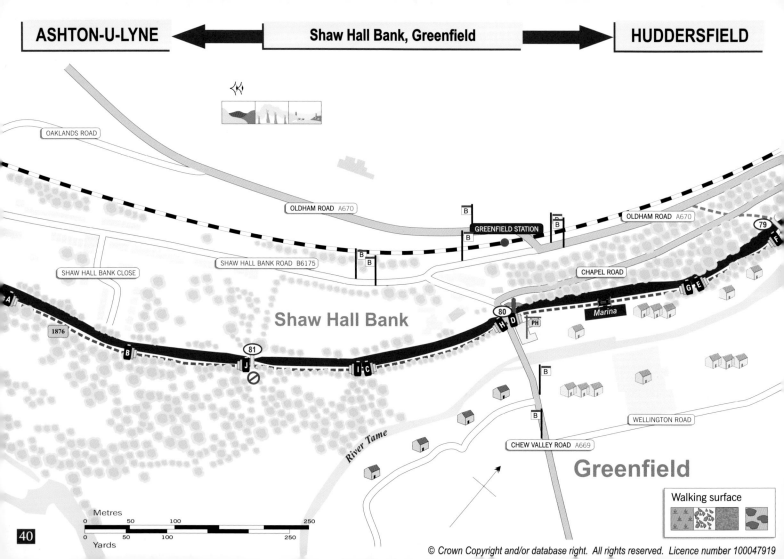

OAKLANDS ROAD

OLDHAM ROAD A670

GREENFIELD STATION

OLDHAM ROAD A670

SHAW HALL BANK ROAD B6175

79

SHAW HALL BANK CLOSE

CHAPEL ROAD

A

G E

1876

Shaw Hall Bank

Marina

B

80

H D

PH

81

J

I C

B

B

WELLINGTON ROAD

CHEW VALLEY ROAD A669

River Tame

**Greenfield**

**Walking surface**

Metres

0     50     100     250

0     50     100     250

Yards

40

## Marks on Stones

The abundance of local Pennine Gritstone meant there was no shortage of building material for the canal. Often the masons' tool marks are still evident and a bold example (❶) can be seen near Lock 20W. The parallel grooves on the surface of the block (❷) in the wall of Lock 5E, show the stone was sawn.

The saw blade was wavy edged and lacked teeth. It was charged with an iron shot abrasive to give the cutting action and left these tell-tale saw marks. The cutting power of abrasives is clearly seen in the deep notches cut into this footbridge stonework (❸) near Lock15E. In the days when horses pulled cargo on the canal, the towing rope, often wet, became rather gritty from lying on the towpath. As the horse hauled its load, the tense, gritty rope would catch against the stonework and gradually grooves were worn into the stone, becoming deeper with years of repetitive wear. Look out for other examples, including those near Lock 1W (worn into iron fenders) and at Lock 20W.

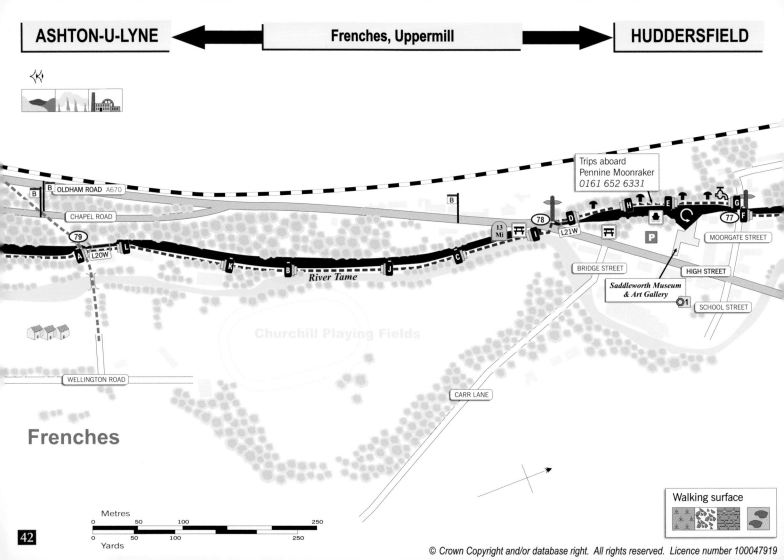

ASHTON-U-LYNE ← Frenches, Uppermill → HUDDERSFIELD

B OLDHAM ROAD A670
B
CHAPEL ROAD
B

Trips aboard
Pennine Moonraker
0161 652 6331

79
A L20W
L

79
K
B
J
River Tame
C
13 Mi
I
78
D
L21W

H
E
G
F
77

P
MOORGATE STREET

BRIDGE STREET
HIGH STREET

Saddleworth Museum
& Art Gallery
1
SCHOOL STREET

Churchill Playing Fields

WELLINGTON ROAD

CARR LANE

Frenches

Walking surface

Metres
0  50  100  250
0  50  100  250
Yards

42

### Saddleworth Museum & Art Gallery

Discover Saddleworth's heritage with exhibitions of landscape and transport, plus a working woollen mill. Award-winning Tourist Information Centre.

*01457 874093*
*Museum Admission Charge*

### Fishing

Sections of the Narrow Canal are well stocked and provide excellent fishing. Particular lengths are controlled by certain angling clubs and require permits to fish. For details, refer to: *www.waterscape.co.uk*

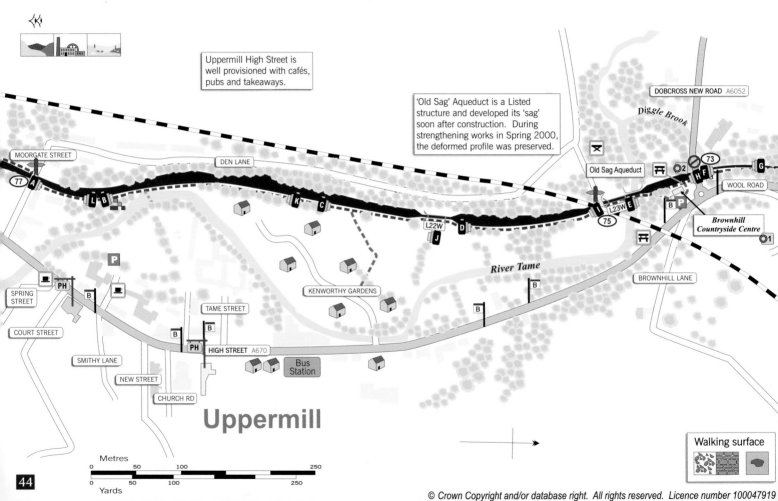

**ASHTON-U-LYNE** ← **Uppermill High Street** → **HUDDERSFIELD**

Uppermill High Street is well provisioned with cafés, pubs and takeaways.

'Old Sag' Aqueduct is a Listed structure and developed its 'sag' soon after construction. During strengthening works in Spring 2000, the deformed profile was preserved.

DOBCROSS NEW ROAD A6052

Diggle Brook

MOORGATE STREET

DEN LANE

77 A

L B

K C

L22W

J

D

Old Sag Aqueduct

75 L23W E

73

F G

WOOL ROAD

2

**Brownhill Countryside Centre**

1

River Tame

SPRING STREET

PH

B

B

COURT STREET

P

B

B

TAME STREET

KENWORTHY GARDENS

B

B

B

BROWNHILL LANE

SMITHY LANE

NEW STREET

PH

HIGH STREET A670

CHURCH RD

Bus Station

## Uppermill

Metres
0   50   100                250

Yards
0   50   100        250

44

Walking surface

### Brownhill Countryside Centre ⊚1

The Centre has a woodland adventure area, changing displays and information on the Tame Valley and its surroundings.

*01457 872598*
*Free Admission*

### Lifting Heavy Stones - II ⊚2

The masonry at Dobcross New Road bridge shows a method of lifting heavy stones. The small depressions cut near the centre of each block (matching depression on the opposite face) were used to locate the pointed jaws of a scissor-action grapple. The heavier the block, the tighter the grip on lifting.

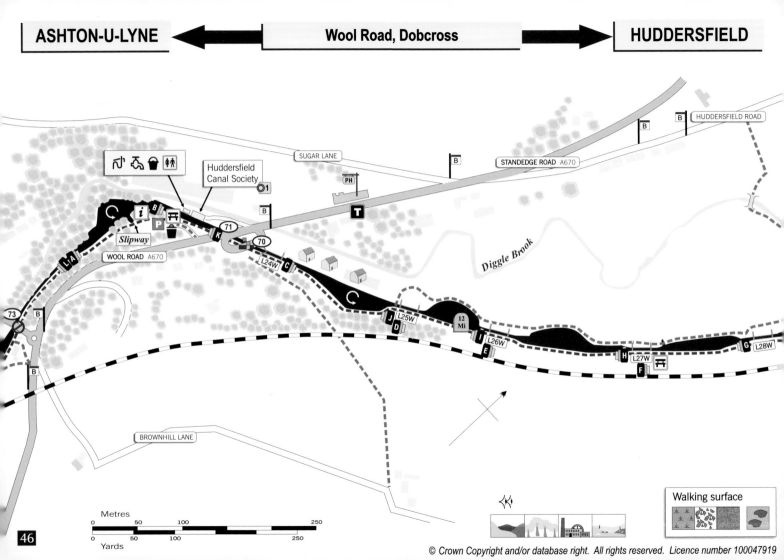

ASHTON-U-LYNE ← Wool Road, Dobcross → HUDDERSFIELD

HUDDERSFIELD ROAD

SUGAR LANE

STANDEDGE ROAD A670

Huddersfield Canal Society

PH

T

Diggle Brook

Slipway

71

70

WOOL ROAD A670

L24W

L25W

L26W

L27W

L28W

12 Mi

73

BROWNHILL LANE

Metres
0   50   100   250

Yards
0   50   100   250

Walking surface

46

### Huddersfield Canal Society 🔵1

Having succeeded in its aim to restore the Huddersfield Narrow Canal to full navigation, it now works to promote the canal's use for the enjoyment of all.

Transhipment Warehouse
Wool Road, Dobcross, Oldham, OL3 5QR
*Tel: 01457 871800*
*EMail: hcs@huddersfieldcanal.com*
*Website: www.huddersfieldcanal.com*

### Locks on the Diggle Flight 🔵2

Possibly a unique arrangement on the waterways network, Locks 25-32W feature single head and tail gates, both hung on the offside, with pairs of inclined paddle gear. The locks were worked entirely from the offside and the design is thought to speed ascent of the flight by horsedrawn boats.

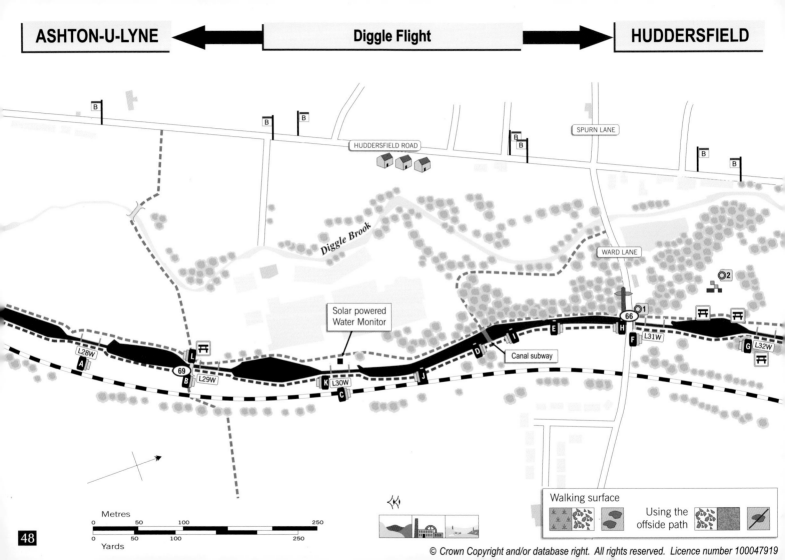

ASHTON-U-LYNE ← Diggle Flight → HUDDERSFIELD

SPURN LANE

HUDDERSFIELD ROAD

*Diggle Brook*

WARD LANE

Solar powered
Water Monitor

Canal subway

L28W
A
L
69
B
L29W
K
L30W
C
J
D
E
I
66
1
2
H
F
L31W
G
L32W

Metres
0    50    100    250

Yards
0    50    100    250

Walking surface
Using the
offside path

48

### Cast Iron Aqueduct ◎1

Easily overlooked, this aqueduct is adjacent to Ward Lane bridge and carries a small stream over the canal to join Diggle Brook. It appears to have been cast in one piece and had made an ideal habitat for a vigorous growth of Marsh Marigold (*Caltha palustris*) when photographed in May 2006.

### Public Art ◎2

These carved wooden heather flowers are part of a Public Art Sculpture Trail commissioned by Oldham Borough Council and installed along the canal. Entitled 'Through Heathered Hills', the piece was designed in association with children from Diggle Primary School.

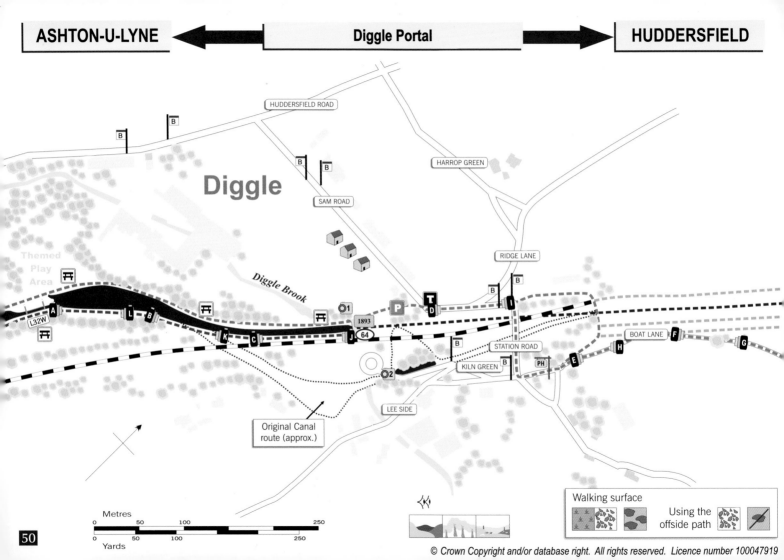

ASHTON-U-LYNE ← Diggle Portal → HUDDERSFIELD

HUDDERSFIELD ROAD

Diggle

HARROP GREEN

SAM ROAD

Diggle Brook

RIDGE LANE

Themed
Play
Area

L32W

1893

64

P

STATION ROAD

KILN GREEN

BOAT LANE

PH

LEE SIDE

Original Canal
route (approx.)

Metres
0    50    100                250

50

0    50    100                250
Yards

Walking surface

Using the
offside path

### *Diggle Portal* ◎1

This entrance to Standedge Tunnel bears the date 1893 showing it to be an extension from the original portal and was built to accommodate the present double track railway line. The modern gates, depicting 'leggers' propelling a narrowboat through the Tunnel, were fitted in April 2006.

### *Original Alignment* ◎2

The building of the first single track railway tunnel in 1849 forced a re-alignment of the canal. The original route was further east, as indicated on the map. A section of this original route, still in water, can be seen at Kiln Green next to the road leading to the bus turning circle.

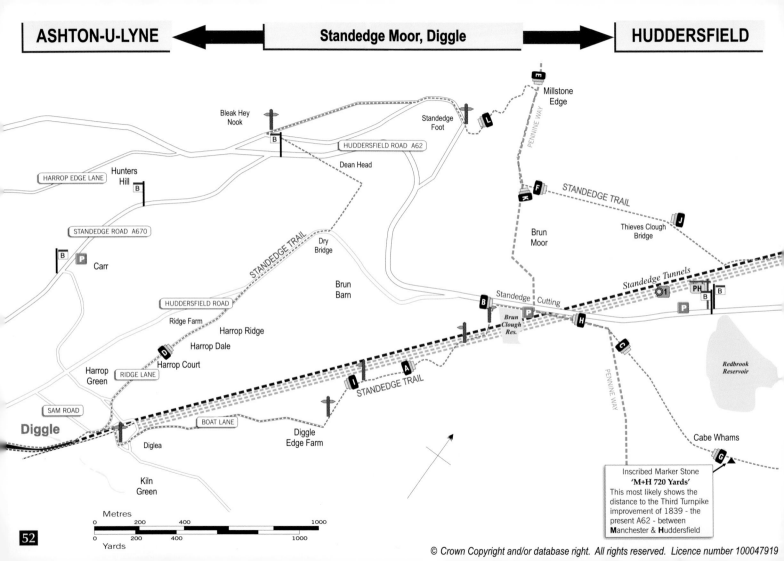

**ASHTON-U-LYNE** ← | Standedge Moor, Diggle | → **HUDDERSFIELD**

m Millstone Edge

Bleak Hey Nook

Standedge Foot

L

B

HUDDERSFIELD ROAD A62

Dean Head

PENNINE WAY

HARROP EDGE LANE

Hunters Hill

B

F

STANDEDGE TRAIL

K

J

Thieves Clough Bridge

Brun Moor

STANDEDGE ROAD A670

Dry Bridge

B
P
Carr

STANDEDGE TRAIL

Brun Barn

Standedge Tunnels

HUDDERSFIELD ROAD

Standedge Cutting

O1

PH

B

Ridge Farm

B

Standedge

I

P

Harrop Ridge

Brun Clough Res.

H

P

Harrop Dale

D

Redbrook Reservoir

Harrop Court

RIDGE LANE

G

Harrop Green

SAM ROAD

STANDEDGE TRAIL

PENNINE WAY

I

A

**Diggle**

BOAT LANE

Diglea

Diggle Edge Farm

Cabe Whams

Kiln Green

G

Metres
0   200   400                    1000

Yards
0   200   400                1000

52

### Inside Standedge Tunnel

Britain's longest canal tunnel at 5200m (4950m as built, but later extended), highest at 196m above sea level and deepest at 194m below the moors. 17 years to build, it opened on the 4th April 1811, finally completing the Ashton to Huddersfield route.

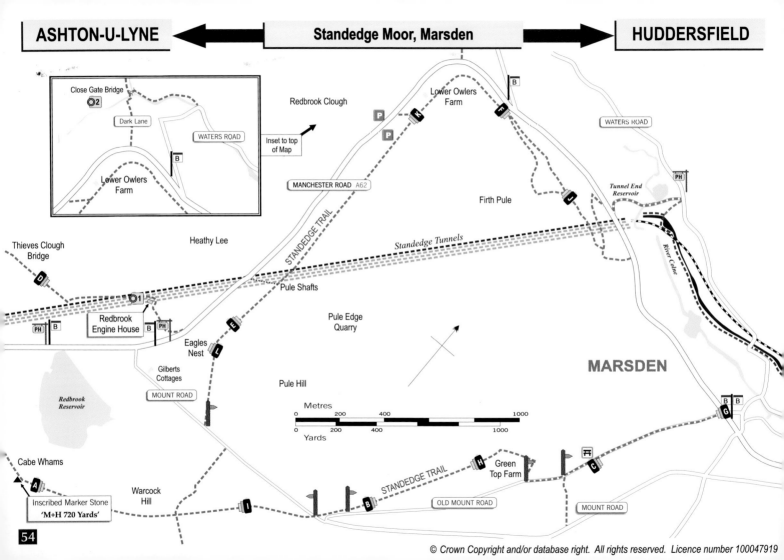

ASHTON-U-LYNE ← Standedge Moor, Marsden → HUDDERSFIELD

**Inset (top left):**

Close Gate Bridge ⊙2
Dark Lane
WATERS ROAD
Inset to top of Map
Lower Owlers Farm
B

**Main map:**

Redbrook Clough

Lower Owlers Farm

P  K  F  B

WATERS ROAD

MANCHESTER ROAD A62

Firth Pule

Tunnel End Reservoir

PH

J

Standedge Tunnels

River Colne

Heathy Lee

STANDEDGE TRAIL

Thieves Clough Bridge

D

Pule Shafts

PH  B  ⊙1  B  PH

Redbrook Engine House

Eagles Nest

E

L

Gilberts Cottages

MOUNT ROAD

Pule Edge Quarry

Pule Hill

MARSDEN

B  B
G

Redbrook Reservoir

Metres
0    200    400    1000

0    200    400    1000
Yards

Cabe Whams

A

Inscribed Marker Stone 'M+H 720 Yards'

Warcock Hill

STANDEDGE TRAIL

H

Green Top Farm

C

I    B    OLD MOUNT ROAD    MOUNT ROAD

**54**

### *Redbrook Engine House* ⓞ1

An impressive Listed structure which housed a large steam engine during tunnelling works, draining the vast quantities of groundwater encountered. The Canal Society's restoration subsidiary, HCS Restoration Ltd, restored and repointed the derelict building in 1993.

### *Close Gate Bridge* ⓞ2

This elegant stone-built bridge is thought to date from the 17th Century. It lies on the old packhorse route from Rochdale to Marsden and is also known locally as Eastergate Bridge. Access via Dark Lane is very steep, muddy when wet and involves a stream crossing using informal stepping stones. TAKE CARE!

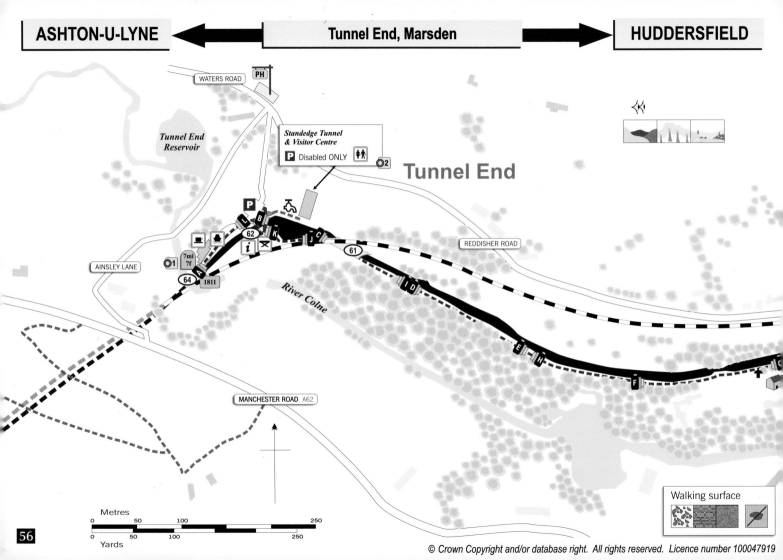

WATERS ROAD

PH

**Tunnel End Reservoir**

*Standedge Tunnel & Visitor Centre*

P Disabled ONLY ⚲2

**Tunnel End**

REDDISHER ROAD

L B
K
62
J C
7mi
7f
i
61
AINSLEY LANE
⚲1
64 A
1811

D

*River Colne*

E

F

MANCHESTER ROAD A62

Metres
0    50    100                    250

Yards
0    50    100              250

Walking surface

56

### 7m 7f Milestone

The milestone commemorates the life of Mr Andrew Charles Hugh Dobson, an active supporter of the Canal Society's early restoration campaign.

### Standedge Visitor Centre

This impressive Canal Warehouse has been used as a 'Magnesia Works' before being converted in 1893 to a canal workshop. It opened as a Visitor Centre in 2001 to coincide with the completed restoration of the Huddersfield Narrow.

01484 844298    www.standedge.co.uk
Free Admission

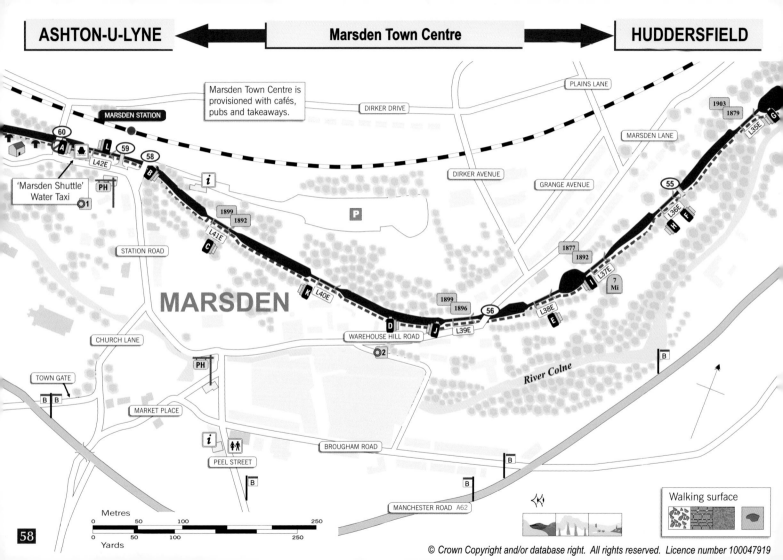

ASHTON-U-LYNE ← Marsden Town Centre → HUDDERSFIELD

PLAINS LANE

DIRKER DRIVE

MARSDEN STATION

Marsden Town Centre is provisioned with cafés, pubs and takeaways.

MARSDEN LANE

1903
1879

L35E

60

A

L

59

58

B

L42E

DIRKER AVENUE

GRANGE AVENUE

55

L36E

F

H

'Marsden Shuttle' Water Taxi

PH

1

i

P

1899
1892

1877
1892

L41E

C

L37E

7 Mi

I

STATION ROAD

MARSDEN

K

L40E

1899
1896

56

L38E

E

B

D

J

L39E

River Colne

CHURCH LANE

WAREHOUSE HILL ROAD

2

TOWN GATE

PH

B B

MARKET PLACE

i

B

Metres

PEEL STREET

B

B

0   50   100                 250

Yards

MANCHESTER ROAD   A62

Walking surface

0   50   100                 250

BROUGHAM ROAD

### Marsden Shuttle ⓞ1

Volunteers from the Huddersfield Canal Society operate a water taxi service between Marsden Station and the Visitor Centre most weekends and Bank Holidays from Easter to the end of October.

*Further information: 01457 871800*

### Stone tenter posts ⓞ2

The Colne Valley was long associated with wool weaving. The cloth was woven untreated and cleaned in Fulling Mills. To pull the wet cloth back to size, it was stretched on to hooked frames or 'tenters'. These unusual stone 'tenter posts' held a frame with beams in the upper and lower elongated slots for the stretching action.

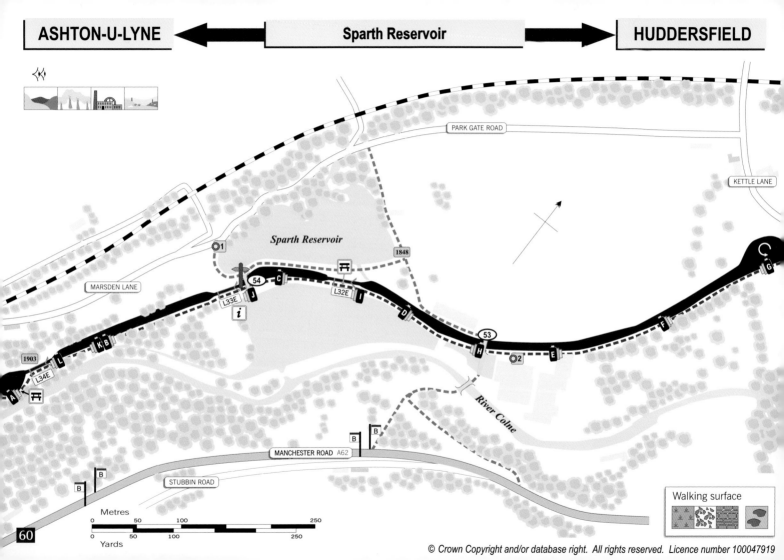

ASHTON-U-LYNE ← Sparth Reservoir → HUDDERSFIELD

Sparth Reservoir

PARK GATE ROAD

KETTLE LANE

1848

MARSDEN LANE

L33E

L32E

54

53

L34E

1903

River Colne

MANCHESTER ROAD A62

STUBBIN ROAD

Metres
0    50    100    250

Yards
0    50    100    250

60

Walking surface

### Sparth Reservoir ◎1

Adequate water was a priority when the canal was constructed and ten reservoirs were built, with a total capacity of about 340 million gallon (1,546 million litre). Today, their contribution to the canal is minimal and the bulk of the water supply is pumped from Scammonden, entering the canal near Lock 42E.

### A Sense of Style ◎2

Retaining walls are often strengthened by a system of bracing wall plates and connecting rods. Nowadays, the 'plates' are plain rectangles of steel, but at Cellars Clough Mill, our forebears believed style should prevail! Others in the same wall show a progression of design to the more functional.

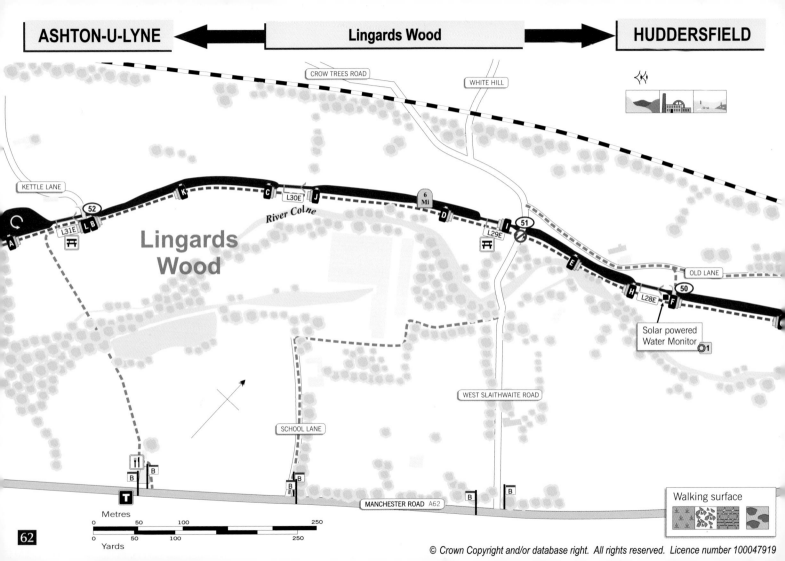

ASHTON-U-LYNE ← Lingards Wood → HUDDERSFIELD

CROW TREES ROAD

WHITE HILL

KETTLE LANE

52

L31E L B

A

**Lingards Wood**

*River Colne*

K

C L30E J

6 Mi

D

51

L29E

E

H L28E F

50

OLD LANE

Solar powered
Water Monitor ○1

WEST SLAITHWAITE ROAD

SCHOOL LANE

T

B B

B B

B

B

MANCHESTER ROAD A62

Metres
0 50 100 250

Yards
0 50 100 250

62

Walking surface

### New Bridge Plates

When the London & North Western Railway Company took over ownership of the Canal, they numbered all the canal bridges and aqueducts with oval metal plates. Over time, all the plates have been lost. Recently, the Society sponsored the re-casting of similar plates and restored the numbering.

### Water Monitor

British Waterways have installed several solar-powered water monitors on the Huddersfield Narrow to record the number of lockages and the bywash flow.

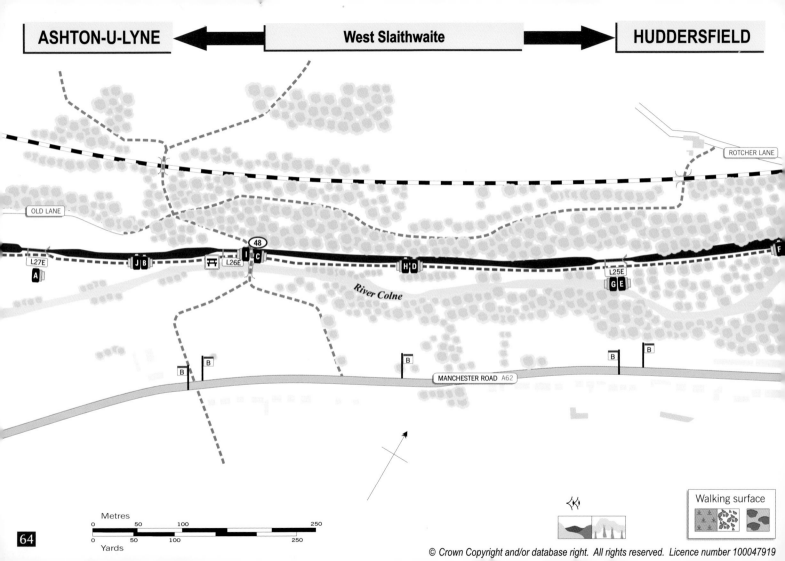

ASHTON-U-LYNE ← West Slaithwaite → HUDDERSFIELD

ROTCHER LANE

OLD LANE

48

L27E

A

J B

L26E

I C

H D

River Colne

L25E

G E

F

MANCHESTER ROAD A62

B

B

B

B

B

Walking surface

Metres
0 50 100 250

Yards
0 50 100 250

64

© Crown Copyright and/or database right. All rights reserved. Licence number 100047919

### Male Fern

The canal wash walls are an ideal habitat for a variety of Ferns. One of the more commonly seen is the Male Fern (*Dryopteris felix-mas*) with tufts of *unbranched* fronds looking rather like a shuttlecock. An oil, extracted from its root-like rhizomes, has been effective in treating tapeworm infections!

### Royal Fern

Look out for the Royal Fern (*Osmunda regalis*) with its characteristic leaf shape and fertile fronds bearing spore-producing structures (sporangia) which ripen to a rust brown colour from June to August.

### Hartstongue

The Hartstongue (*Phyllitis scolopendrium*) is easily recognisable as our only fern with evergreen, strap-like fronds. Often the fronds have a pleated appearance marking the long sporangia on the underside which ripen from August, through the Winter, to early Spring.

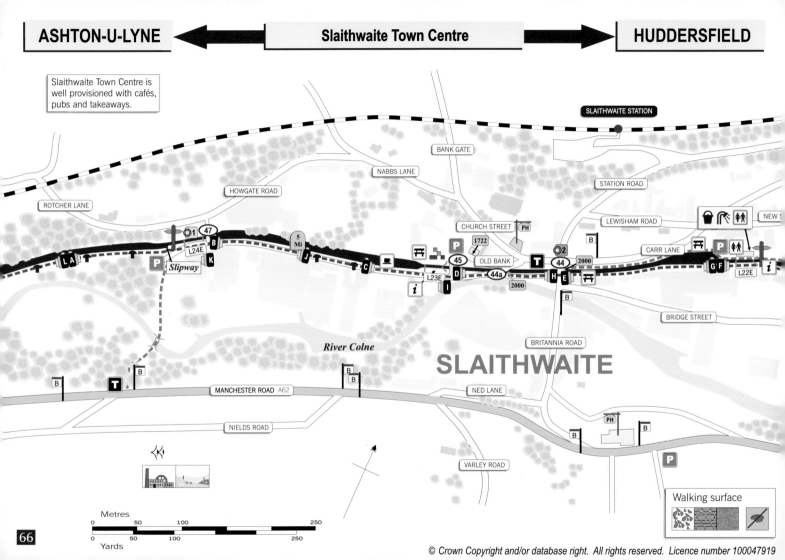

### Lock 24E ◎1

The guillotine tail gate at Lock 24E is unique on a narrow canal. Restoration of this lock was the Canal Society's last major scheme; completed Spring 1998.

### Slaithwaite Restoration ◎2

Restoring the canal through Slaithwaite town centre was a major engineering project. The view is from Britannia Road looking east.

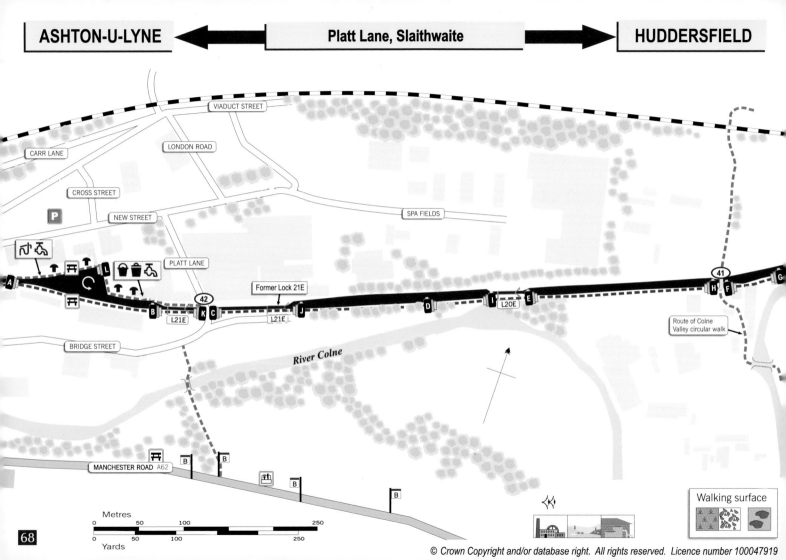

ASHTON-U-LYNE ← Platt Lane, Slaithwaite → HUDDERSFIELD

VIADUCT STREET
CARR LANE
LONDON ROAD
CROSS STREET
P
NEW STREET
SPA FIELDS
PLATT LANE
A
L
42
Former Lock 21E
B
L21E
K C
L21E
J
D
I
L20E
E
41
H F
G
BRIDGE STREET
Route of Colne
Valley circular walk
River Colne
MANCHESTER ROAD A62
B
B
B
B

Metres
0    50    100    250
Yards
0    50    100    250

Walking surface

68

### Relics of the Past ...

Water Horsetail (*Equisetum fluviatile*) growing through the broad leaves of Water Plantain (*Alisma plantago-aquatica*). Giant relatives of the Horsetail dominated forest vegetation during Carboniferous times (320 million years ago) and their preserved remains formed the coal deposits mined today.

A specimen of Ginkgo or the Maidenhair Tree (*Ginkgo biloba*) may be seen at Lock 23E. It has remained almost unchanged since Jurassic times (180 million years ago) and fossilised fragments of its leaves *(inset)* may be found in rocks on the Yorkshire coast.

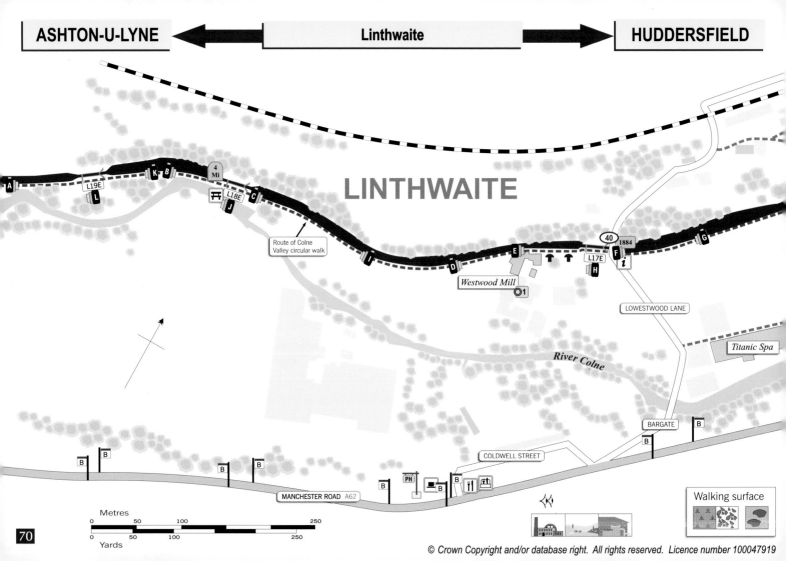

ASHTON-U-LYNE ← Linthwaite → HUDDERSFIELD

LINTHWAITE

4 Mi

L19E

L18E

Route of Colne Valley circular walk

Westwood Mill

40 1884

L17E

LOWESTWOOD LANE

Titanic Spa

River Colne

BARGATE

COLDWELL STREET

MANCHESTER ROAD A62

Metres
0    50    100    250

Yards
50    100    250

70

Walking surface

### Westwood Mill 　　①1

Also referred to as Low Westwood Mill, these listed buildings are believed to be the oldest surviving woollen mill complex in the Colne Valley; pre-dating the construction of the Canal. Records show a Fulling Mill was on the site as early as 1604 confirming the importance of this early industrial site.

### Datestones

You will encounter a lot of different datestones along the Canal. Many commemorate the re-building of original canal structures, such as a lock chamber wall (*pictured*) or the building of a stone bridge to replace an earlier wooden swing bridge which had fallen into disrepair.

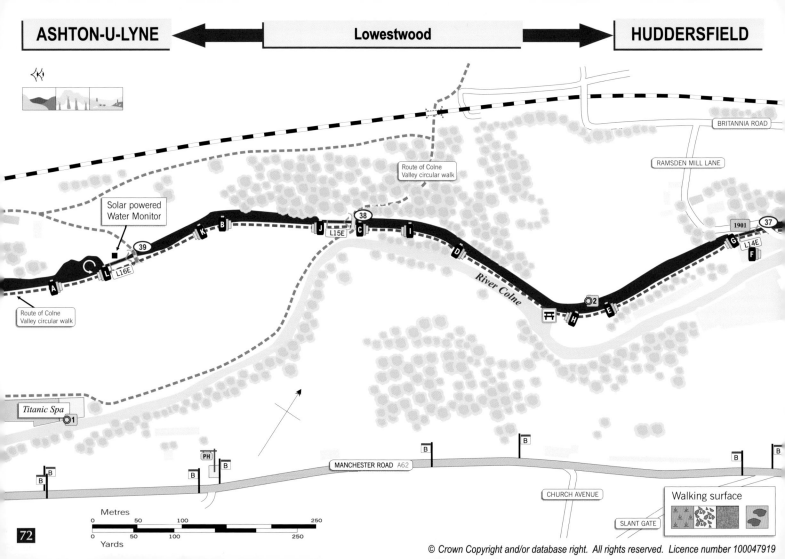

ASHTON-U-LYNE ← Lowestwood → HUDDERSFIELD

Solar powered
Water Monitor

39

L16E

A

L

B

J

L15E

38

C

I

D

Route of Colne
Valley circular walk

River Colne

2

H

E

G

L14E

F

1901

37

BRITANNIA ROAD

RAMSDEN MILL LANE

Route of Colne
Valley circular walk

Titanic Spa

1

PH

B

B

B

B

B

B

B

MANCHESTER ROAD  A62

CHURCH AVENUE

SLANT GATE

Walking surface

Metres
0    50    100              250

Yards
0    50    100              250

72

### Titanic Spa & Apartments ⊙1

Lowestwood Mill was originally built for the Colne Valley Spinning Company in 1911, but soon gained the nickname 'Titanic Mill' after the launch of the ill-fated liner, RMS Titanic, the same year. The mill has been converted to a health spa, hotel and apartments, and has maintained its imposing presence.

### Fringed Water Lily ⊙2

The Fringed Water-lily (*Nymphoides peltatus*) takes its name from its fringed petals (*inset*). A colony may be seen in the pound between Locks 14 & 15E. Despite the name and 'lily pad' leaves, it is not a true Water-lily, but a member of the Bogbean Family.

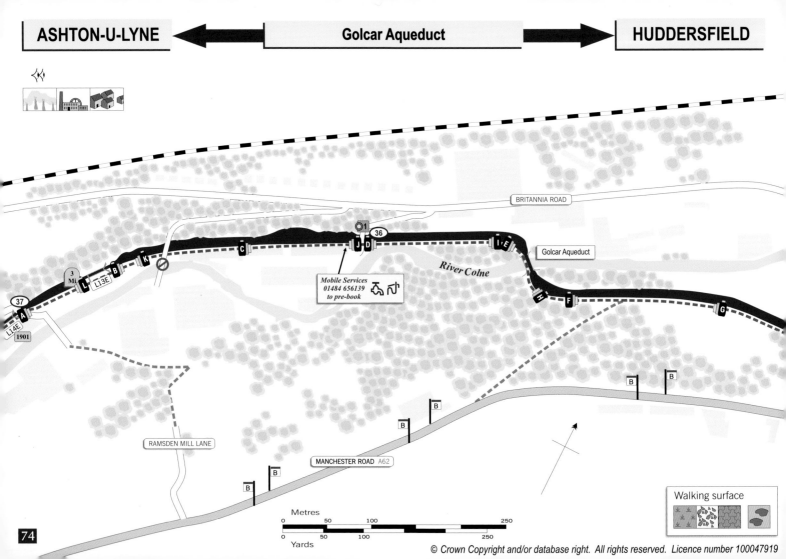

ASHTON-U-LYNE

Golcar Aqueduct

HUDDERSFIELD

BRITANNIA ROAD

Golcar Aqueduct

River Colne

Mobile Services
01484 656139
to pre-book

3 Mi
L13E
L14E
1901

37
A

36
J D
I E
H F
G

RAMSDEN MILL LANE

MANCHESTER ROAD   A62

Walking surface

Metres
0    50    100                    250
0    50    100         250
Yards

74

### *Holme Mill Bridge* 📷1

This view, from September 1998, shows the former fixed swing-bridge at Holme Mill. Built in the 1920s as a more heavy duty crossing for Holme Mill, the steelwork was removed during restoration and now 'lies in state' on Standedge Moor.

### *White-Clawed Crayfish*

During the restoration work at Holme Mill Bridge, White-clawed Crayfish were discovered in the canal. They were rescued, transferred to an undisturbed section of canal nearby and reintroduced once the new bridge was completed. The work included installing submerged 'cavity bricks' - ideal crayfish homes!

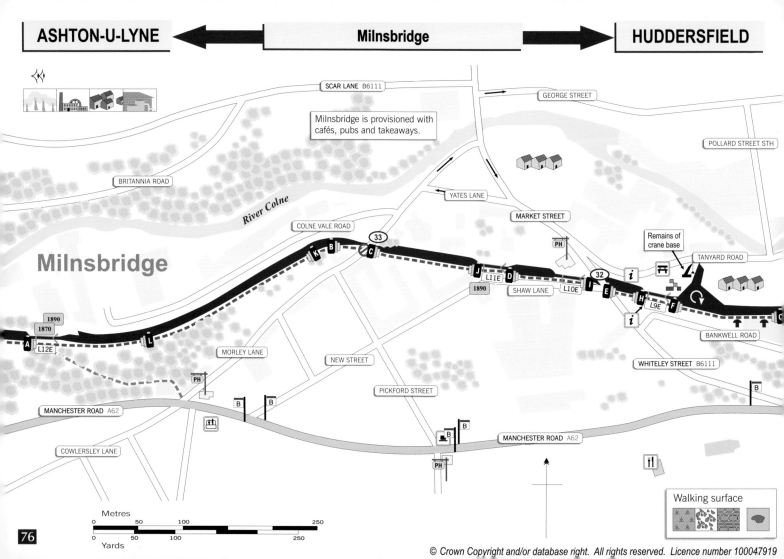

ASHTON-U-LYNE ← Milnsbridge → HUDDERSFIELD

SCAR LANE B6111

GEORGE STREET

POLLARD STREET STH

Milnsbridge is provisioned with cafés, pubs and takeaways.

BRITANNIA ROAD

River Colne

COLNE VALE ROAD

YATES LANE

MARKET STREET

Remains of crane base

TANYARD ROAD

33

PH

**Milnsbridge**

K B
C

J
L11E D
L10E
1890
SHAW LANE

32
I E
H
L9E F
C

BANKWELL ROAD

1890
1870

A
L12E

L

MORLEY LANE

NEW STREET

WHITELEY STREET B6111

B

PH
B B
PICKFORD STREET

MANCHESTER ROAD A62

COWLERSLEY LANE

B B
PH

MANCHESTER ROAD A62

76

Metres
0 50 100 250

0 50 100 250
Yards

Walking surface

### Gardens in miniature - Mosses & Lichens

The stone boundary walls along the towpath are an ideal habitat for many different types of moss and lichen. Lichens are unusual being a partnership between an alga and a fungus.

They show a wonderful variety of forms including patches of colour, incrustations and 'leafy' clumps.

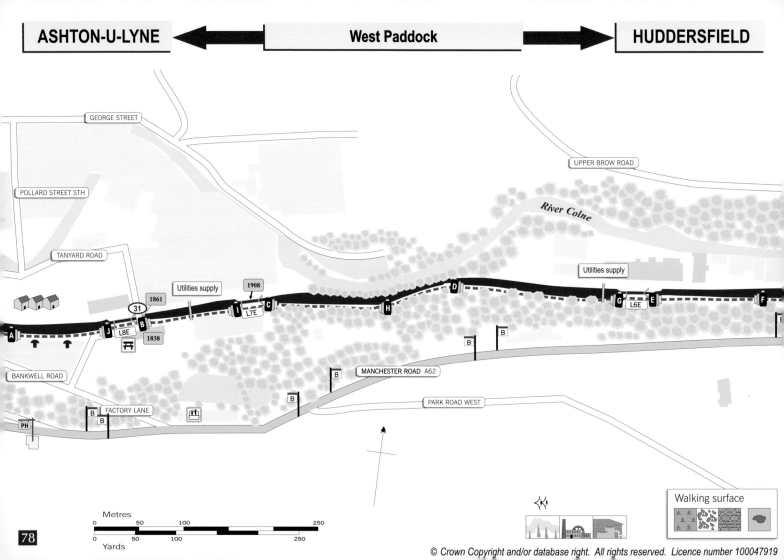

ASHTON-U-LYNE ← West Paddock → HUDDERSFIELD

GEORGE STREET

UPPER BROW ROAD

POLLARD STREET STH

*River Colne*

TANYARD ROAD

Utilities supply

1861

31

Utilities supply

1908

B

C

L7E

D

G

L6E

E

F

A

J

L8E

1838

H

B

B

B

BANKWELL ROAD

B

MANCHESTER ROAD  A62

B

PARK ROAD WEST

B

FACTORY LANE

B

PH

Metres
0    50    100    250

Yards
0    50    100    250

Walking surface

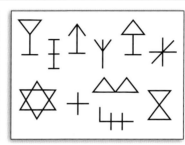

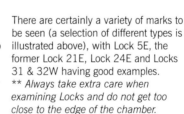

## *Mason Marks*

Blocks of stone, especially those used to construct the lock walls, were accurately cut and finished to a smooth surface. Often you see designs cut into the block, made up of a combination of straight, or more rarely curved, chisel cuts. These marks are collectively known as Mason Marks and are

generally thought to be the 'signatures' of particular stonemasons, identifying their work and allowing their payment to be calculated. It has also been suggested that the marks may refer to a particular quarry supplying the stone, or contain information for the correct setting out of the lock wall construction.

There are certainly a variety of marks to be seen (a selection of different types is illustrated above), with Lock 5E, the former Lock 21E, Lock 24E and Locks 31 & 32W having good examples.
** *Always take extra care when examining Locks and do not get too close to the edge of the chamber.*

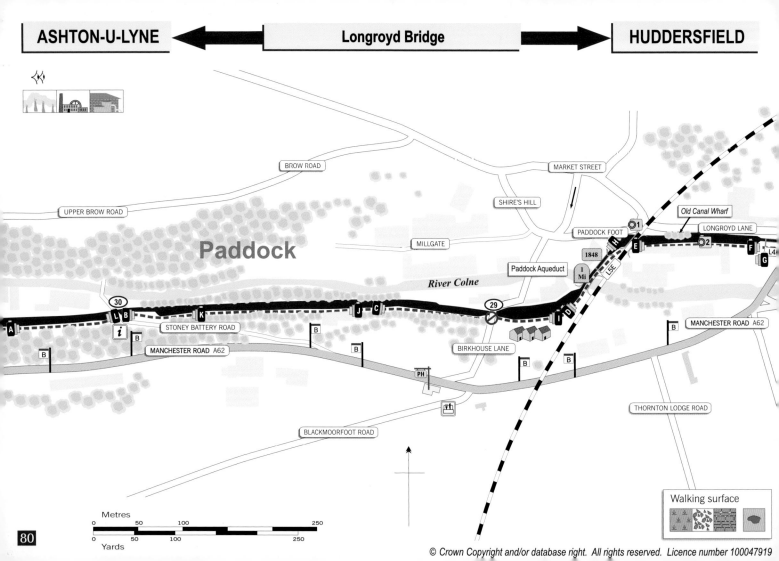

ASHTON-U-LYNE ← **Longroyd Bridge** → HUDDERSFIELD

Paddock

BROW ROAD

UPPER BROW ROAD

MARKET STREET

SHIRE'S HILL

MILLGATE

*Old Canal Wharf*

PADDOCK FOOT

○1

○2

LONGROYD LANE

1848

Paddock Aqueduct

1 Mi

*River Colne*

L5E

30

L B

K

J C

29

I D

E

F
L4
G

*i*

STONEY BATTERY ROAD

B

B

B

B

BIRKHOUSE LANE

B

B

MANCHESTER ROAD A62

MANCHESTER ROAD A62

PH

THORNTON LODGE ROAD

BLACKMOORFOOT ROAD

Metres
0    50    100    250

80

Yards
0    50    100    250

Walking surface

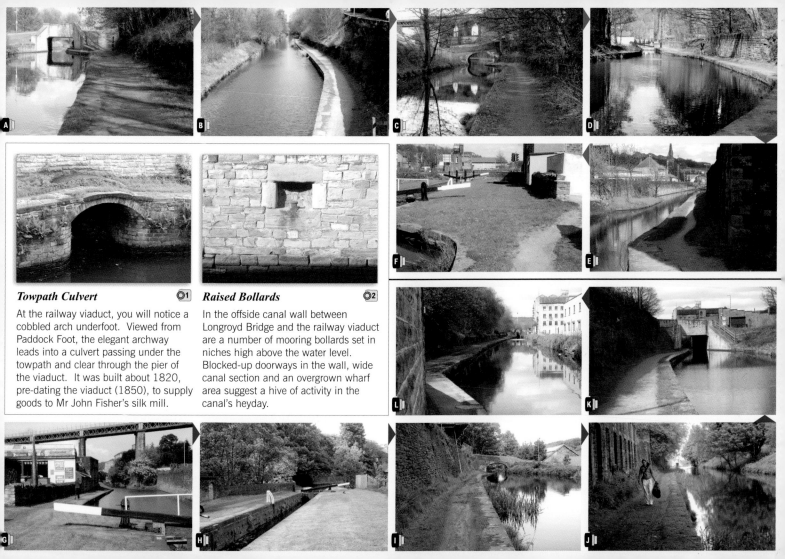

## Towpath Culvert ◎1

At the railway viaduct, you will notice a cobbled arch underfoot. Viewed from Paddock Foot, the elegant archway leads into a culvert passing under the towpath and clear through the pier of the viaduct. It was built about 1820, pre-dating the viaduct (1850), to supply goods to Mr John Fisher's silk mill.

## Raised Bollards ◎2

In the offside canal wall between Longroyd Bridge and the railway viaduct are a number of mooring bollards set in niches high above the water level. Blocked-up doorways in the wall, wide canal section and an overgrown wharf area suggest a hive of activity in the canal's heyday.

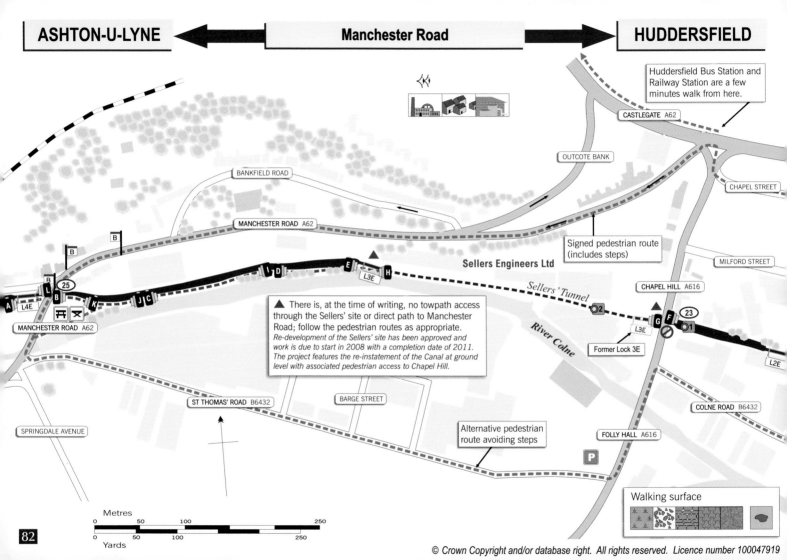

**ASHTON-U-LYNE** ← **Manchester Road** → **HUDDERSFIELD**

Huddersfield Bus Station and Railway Station are a few minutes walk from here.

CASTLEGATE A62

OUTCOTE BANK

CHAPEL STREET

BANKFIELD ROAD

MANCHESTER ROAD A62

Signed pedestrian route (includes steps)

MILFORD STREET

Sellers Engineers Ltd

Sellers' Tunnel

CHAPEL HILL A616

River Colne

Former Lock 3E

L2E

▲ There is, at the time of writing, no towpath access through the Sellers' site or direct path to Manchester Road; follow the pedestrian routes as appropriate. *Re-development of the Sellers' site has been approved and work is due to start in 2008 with a completion date of 2011. The project features the re-instatement of the Canal at ground level with associated pedestrian access to Chapel Hill.*

MANCHESTER ROAD A62

B

25

L4E

A

L

B

K

J

C

D

I

E

L3E

H

G

F

23

L3E

FOLLY HALL A616

COLNE ROAD B6432

SPRINGDALE AVENUE

ST THOMAS' ROAD B6432

BARGE STREET

Alternative pedestrian route avoiding steps

P

Walking surface

Metres
0    50    100    250

Yards
0    50    100    250

82

A

B

C

D

F

E

## *Chapel Hill* ⊙1

This aerial view, taken in April 1991, shows Chapel Hill running across the picture, the canal in the centre and the River Colne to the left. The Sellers Engineers' site, beyond Chapel Hill, shows the planned restoration route of the canal was largely unobstructed.

## *Constructing Sellers' Tunnel* ⊙2

To maintain the operation of the works, a tunnel through the Sellers' site was constructed using the 'cut and cover' method; excavating the canal channel and then capping with concrete. Ironically, the Sellers' site is now being re-developed and the canal will be re-instated at surface level.

L

K

G

H

I

J

**HUDDERSFIELD**

HUDDERSFIELD
TOWN CENTRE
All services

QUEENSGATE A62

CHAPEL HILL A616

CHAPEL STREET

MILFORD STREET

▲ There is no towpath access through the Bates & Co. site; follow the pedestrian routes as appropriate

QUEEN STREET SOUTH

L2E

Bates & Co.

◎1

22 △ A

COLNE ROAD B6432

L2E

Former Lock 2E

Signed pedestrian route (includes steps)

Huddersfield University

Solar powered Water Monitor

1871  21  Huddersfield Narrow Canal

K B

FIRTH STREET B6432

L1E  C

J

D

◎2

Huddersfield Broad Canal

I E

H

Aspley Basin

F

G

ST ANDREW'S ROAD B6432

Aspley Wharf Marina Ltd
01484 514123

WAKEFIELD ROAD A629

River Colne

Alternative pedestrian route avoiding steps

COMMERCIAL STREET

KING'S BRIDGE ROAD

Walking surface

Metres
0    50    100    250

Yards
0    50    100    250

84

### Queen Street South Bridge ⊙1

Restoring the canal through the Bates site involved creating a new tunnel under the buildings, dropping the original canal level by 3m. This would undermine the foundations of Queen St. South bridge and the view above, from within Bates, shows a cement slurry being injected to stabilise the ground.

### Hand Crane & Warehouse ⊙2

The old warehouse at Wakefield Road, reputedly one of the oldest on the canal network, is now converted into residences, but the hand-operated crane still stands in almost original condition. The crane served the warehouse and a former wooden 'bonded' warehouse nearby.

## HUDDERSFIELD CANAL SOCIETY

Having achieved its aim of restoring
the Huddersfield Narrow Canal to full
navigation, the Canal Society continues
to work with its partners: British
Waterways and the local authorities of
Tameside, Oldham and Kirklees, to
promote the use of the Canal for the
enjoyment of all.

If you would like to know more about
the work of the Canal Society, please
contact:

Huddersfield Canal Society
Transhipment Warehouse
Wool Road, Dobcross
OLDHAM, OL3 5QR

*Tel: 01457 871800*
*EMail: hcs@huddersfieldcanal.com*
*Website: www.huddersfieldcanal.com*

## FURTHER INFORMATION

The Huddersfield Narrow Canal is covered by the following Ordnance Survey® maps:

1:50 000 Landranger Series - Maps 109 & 110

1:25 000 Explorer Series - It is best to use their 'OS Select' service to generate canal-centred maps (www.ordnancesurvey.co.uk).

Aerial imagery is now available in the public domain through the Internet (Broadband connection required). Freely accessible services such as Google® Earth and Microsoft® VE give good resolution views of the entire Huddersfield Narrow and though some sections are clearly out of date, they are updated when more recent surveys are made available.

Impartial advice on all forms of public transport serving the region is available from the Traveline (0871 200 2323 www.traveline.org.uk) and for West Yorkshire, Metro (0113 245 7676 www.wymetro.com).

## PHOTO CREDITS

All photographs, the Author, except:

Huddersfield Canal Society
*Pages 12 & 53 - Inside Standedge Tunnel*

Nick Martin
*Page 31 - Heron*
*Page 35 - Wide-bodied Chaser Dragonfly*

Alan Stopher
*Page 23 - Stalybridge Restoration - I*
*Page 67 - Slaithwaite Restoration*
*Page 75 - White-Clawed Crayfish*
*Page 83 - Constructing Sellers' Tunnel*

Steve Turvey
*Page 25 - Branched Bur-reed*

## USEFUL CONTACTS

**British Waterways (NW)**   01942 405700
Waterside Drive, Wigan, WN3 5AZ

**British Waterways (Yorks)**   0113 281 6800
Fearns Wharf, Neptune Street, Leeds, LS9 8PB

**British Waterways' leisure website**
www.waterscape.com

**Brownhill Countryside Centre**   01457 872598
Wool Road, Dobcross, Oldham, OL3 5PB
www.oldham.gov.uk/oldham-countryside-service

**Huddersfield Canal Society**   01457 871800
Wool Road, Dobcross, Oldham, OL3 5QR
www.huddersfieldcanal.com

**Huddersfield TIC**   01484 223200
3-5 Albion Street, Huddersfield, HD1 2NW
www.kirklees.gov.uk/visitorportal/visitorinfo

**Marsden Information Point**   01484 845595
20-26 Peel Street, Marsden, HD7 6BW

**Oldham TIC**   0161 627 1024
12 Albion Street, Oldham, OL1 3BB
www.oldham.gov.uk/community/tourist_information

**Portland Basin Museum**   0161 343 2878
Portland Place, Ashton-u-Lyne, OL7 0QA
www.tameside.gov.uk/museumsgalleries/portland

**Saddleworth Museum**   01457 874093
High Street, Uppermill, Oldham, OL3 6HS
www.saddleworthmuseum.co.uk

**Standedge Visitor Centre**   01484 844298
Waters Road, Marsden, Huddersfield, HD7 6NQ
www.standedge.co.uk

**Tameside TIC**   0161 343 4343
Wellington Road, Ashton-u-Lyne, OL6 6DL
www.tameside.gov.uk/touristinfocentre

## REFERENCES

Automobile Association Developments Ltd., *Street by Street - West Yorkshire*, 1st Ed., 2001

Blamey, M., Fitter, R., & Fitter, A., *Wild Flowers of Britain & Ireland*, A & C Black, 2003

Chinery, M., *A Field Guide to the Insects of Britain & Northern Europe*, Collins, 1984

Civic Trust, *Environmental Audit of the Huddersfield Narrow Canal*, Huddersfield Canal Society, 1992

Ellis, T., *Bridge numbers on the Huddersfield Narrow and Broad Canals*, Personal communication, 2009

Fox, M. & P., *Pennine Passage - The History of the Huddersfield Narrow Canal*, Huddersfield Canal Society, 1989

Geographers' A-Z Company Ltd., *Greater Manchester Street Atlas*, 3rd Ed., 2002

Gibson, K., *Pennine Dreams - The story of the Huddersfield Narrow Canal*, Tempus, 2002

Huddersfield Canal Society, *Towpath Guide*, 1981

Kirklees MC (Countryside Unit), *Colne Valley Circular Walk*, under revision, due 2008

Kirklees MC, *The Standedge Trail*, 2nd Ed.

Saddleworth Historical Society, *Huddersfield Narrow Canal*, Bulletin re-prints, 1994

*A Book of the all the Acts Proceedings and Transactions of the Committee of the Huddersfield Canal Company*, (1796-1843)

*London & North Western Railway Company. Huddersfield Canals.  Minute Book* (1855-1869)

# TOWPATH DISTANCE TABLE - WEST

## How to use these Tables

To find the distance between any two places listed, read across the row for the place lowest in the list until you reach the column for the second place and the resulting figure will be the distance in km.

Examples:

Lock 1W to Grove Road is 4.44km
Lock 42E to Golcar Aqueduct is 7.77km

| Place | Lock 1W, Whitelands | Lock 2W, Plantation Street | Clarence Street, Whitelands | Tame Aqueduct | Caroline Street, Stalybridge | Mottram Road, Stalybridge | Grove Road, Heyrod | Lock 10W, Heyrod | Scout Tunnel (West portal) | Scout Tunnel (East portal) | Egmont Street, Mossley | Lock 14W, Woodend | Manchester Road, Roaches | Well-i-Hole Road | Chew Valley Road, Greenfield | High Street, Uppermill | Wool Road, Dobcross | Ward Lane, Diggle | Diggle Portal |
|---|---|---|---|---|---|---|---|---|---|---|---|---|---|---|---|---|---|---|---|
| Ward Lane, Diggle | | | | | | | | | | | | | | | | | | | 0.51 |
| Wool Road, Dobcross | | | | | | | | | | | | | | | | | | 1.27 | 1.78 |
| High Street, Uppermill | | | | | | | | | | | | | | | | | 1.28 | 2.55 | 3.06 |
| Chew Valley Road, Greenfield | | | | | | | | | | | | | | | | 0.87 | 2.15 | 3.41 | 3.93 |
| Well-i-Hole Road | | | | | | | | | | | | | | | 0.87 | 1.74 | 3.02 | 4.29 | 4.80 |
| Manchester Road, Roaches | | | | | | | | | | | | | | 1.13 | 2.00 | 2.87 | 4.15 | 5.42 | 5.93 |
| Lock 14W, Woodend | | | | | | | | | | | | | 0.97 | 2.10 | 2.97 | 3.84 | 5.12 | 6.39 | 6.90 |
| Egmont Street, Mossley | | | | | | | | | | | | 0.83 | 1.80 | 2.93 | 3.80 | 4.67 | 5.95 | 7.22 | 7.73 |
| Scout Tunnel (East portal) | | | | | | | | | | | 0.75 | 1.58 | 2.55 | 3.68 | 4.55 | 5.42 | 6.70 | 7.97 | 8.48 |
| Scout Tunnel (West portal) | | | | | | | | | | 0.19 | 0.94 | 1.77 | 2.74 | 3.87 | 4.74 | 5.61 | 6.89 | 8.16 | 8.67 |
| Lock 10W, Heyrod | | | | | | | | | 0.55 | 0.74 | 1.49 | 2.32 | 3.29 | 4.42 | 5.29 | 6.16 | 7.44 | 8.71 | 9.22 |
| Grove Road, Heyrod | | | | | | | | 0.64 | 1.19 | 1.38 | 2.13 | 2.96 | 3.93 | 5.06 | 5.93 | 6.80 | 8.08 | 9.35 | 9.86 |
| Mottram Road, Stalybridge | | | | | | | 1.61 | 2.25 | 2.80 | 2.99 | 3.74 | 4.57 | 5.54 | 6.67 | 7.54 | 8.41 | 9.69 | 10.96 | 11.47 |
| Caroline Street, Stalybridge | | | | | | 0.81 | 2.42 | 3.06 | 3.61 | 3.80 | 4.55 | 5.38 | 6.35 | 7.48 | 8.35 | 9.22 | 10.50 | 11.77 | 12.28 |
| Tame Aqueduct | | | | | 0.62 | 143 | 3.04 | 3.68 | 4.23 | 4.42 | 5.17 | 6.00 | 6.97 | 8.10 | 8.97 | 9.84 | 11.12 | 12.39 | 12.90 |
| Clarence Street, Whitelands | | | | 0.36 | 0.98 | 1.79 | 3.40 | 4.04 | 4.59 | 4.78 | 5.53 | 6.36 | 7.33 | 8.46 | 9.33 | 10.20 | 11.48 | 12.75 | 13.26 |
| Lock 2W, Plantation Street | | | 0.51 | 0.87 | 1.49 | 2.30 | 3.91 | 4.55 | 5.10 | 5.29 | 6.04 | 6.87 | 7.84 | 8.97 | 9.84 | 10.71 | 11.99 | 13.26 | 13.77 |
| Lock 1W, Whitelands | | 0.53 | 1.04 | 1.40 | 2.02 | 2.83 | 4.44 | 5.08 | 5.63 | 5.82 | 6.57 | 7.40 | 8.37 | 9.50 | 10.37 | 11.24 | 12.52 | 13.79 | 14.30 |
| Portland Basin, Ashton-u-Lyne | 0.93 | 1.46 | 1.97 | 2.33 | 2.95 | 3.76 | 5.37 | 6.01 | 6.56 | 6.75 | 7.50 | 8.33 | 9.30 | 10.43 | 11.30 | 12.17 | 13.45 | 14.72 | 15.23 |

Conversion Scale

Km 0 — 1 — 2 — 3 — 4 — 5 — 6 — 7 — 8
Mi 0 — 1 — 2 — 3 — 4 — 5